Big City Politics

STUDIES IN POLITICAL SCIENCE

Random House   New York

BIG CITY POLITICS

◄●►

A Comparative Guide to the Political Systems of

ATLANTA	EL PASO	PHILADELPHIA
BOSTON	LOS ANGELES	ST. LOUIS
DETROIT	MIAMI	SEATTLE

EDWARD C. BANFIELD

HARVARD UNIVERSITY

Second Printing, May 1966
© Copyright, 1965, by Random House, Inc.
All rights reserved under International and Pan-American Copyright
Conventions. Published in New York by Random House, Inc. and
simultaneously in Toronto, Canada, by Random House of Canada Limited.
Library of Congress Catalog Card Number: 65–13765
Manufactured in the United States of America
by H. Wolff, New York

A Note on Authorship

This book has an author in the sense that one person decided on its plan, put its language in final form, and takes responsibility for everything in it. In another sense, however, it has nine authors and an editor-compiler. The principal source of each chapter was a report in the series published by the Joint Center for Urban Studies of the Massachusetts Institute of Technology and Harvard University. The author wishes to express his appreciation to the authors of these reports (they are listed below) and to the Joint Center for its generous support of this undertaking. Appreciation is also due Mark K. Adams, Martha Derthick, and Mitchell Grodzins, who gave editorial assistance. Information to supplement the Joint Center reports on some points was obtained by the author through interviews with politicians in Atlanta, Boston, Detroit, El Paso, and Los Angeles. Additional information was obtained through interviews conducted by students and from published sources; to the student volunteers (also listed below) particular thanks are due. Obviously the authors of the original reports cannot be held responsible for a product that has passed through so many hands; the author assumes sole responsibility for it.

In the following listing, the name of the author of the Joint Center report is given immediately after the name of the city.

Atlanta. Kenneth E. Gray. Mr. Gray was prevented from completing his report on Atlanta; however, his notes were the principal source of the chapter that appears here. Wayne Kelley and Raleigh Bryans provided additional information. See also M. Kent Jennings, *Community Influentials,* The Free Press of Glencoe, New York, 1964; Jack L. Walker, "Protest and Negotiation: A Case Study of Negro Leadership in Atlanta, Georgia," *Midwest Journal of Political Science,* VII (May, 1963); Seymour Freedgood, "Life in Buckhead," *Fortune,* September, 1961; James L. Townsend,

"What Sort of a Mayor?," *Atlanta Magazine,* January, 1962, and Eugene Patterson, "The Making of a Mayor," *Atlanta Magazine,* November, 1963.

Boston. The Joint Center report was the product of a graduate seminar at Harvard and was edited by E. C. Banfield and Martha Derthick. A section of this report by Peter Braestrup dealing with the Boston press appeared in abbreviated form in *Harper's,* October, 1960.

Detroit. David Greenstone. See also Tom Nicholson, "Detroit's Surprising Mayor," *Harper's,* December, 1963.

El Paso. Mark and Gertrude Adams.

Los Angeles. James Q. Wilson. See also James Phelan, "Trouble in Happyland," *Saturday Evening Post,* May 25, 1963; Charles G. Mayo, "The Mass Media and Campaign Strategy in a Mayoralty Election," *Journalism Quarterly,* 41:3 (Summer 1964) and "The 1961 Mayoralty Election in Los Angeles: The Political Party in a Nonpartisan Election," *The Western Political Quarterly,* XVII:2 (June 1964), and *The Los Angeles Newsletter.*

Miami (Dade County). Edward Sofen. Clarence Jones provided additional information.

Philadelphia. Robert L. Freedman. William A. Humenuk provided additional information. See also James Reichley, *The Art of Government: Reform and Organization Politics in Philadelphia,* Fund for the Republic, New York, 1959.

Seattle. Charles W. Bender. Charles L. Jackson and David D. Tripple provided additional information.

St. Louis. Kenneth E. Gray. Leonard Strauss, Jr. provided additional information. See also Robert H. Salisbury, "St. Louis Politics: A Note on Relationships Among Interests, Parties, and Governmental Structure," *Western Political Quarterly,* June, 1960, and "The Dynamics of Reform: Charter Politics in St. Louis," *Midwest Journal of Political Science,* August, 1961. Also H. J. Schmandt, P. G. Steinbicker, and G. D. Wendel, *Metropolitan Reform in St. Louis,* Holt, Rinehart and Winston, New York, 1962.

Contents

————◄●►————

Big City Politics

Introduction

The obstacles in the way of solving city problems (insofar as "solutions" exist) are mainly political. Slums, racial injustice, traffic congestion, inadequate schools, air pollution—there is not an item on the whole familiar list that is a problem solely, or even primarily, for lack of resources, technical knowledge, or organization. In each case the main thing that stands in the way of remedial action is conflict. People's interests and opinions differ, and therefore they disagree about what, if anything, is to be done. Politics is the process by which conflict is carried on in matters of public concern, and the political system of a city is the set of formal and informal arrangements (laws, offices, interest groups, voting procedures, and so on) by which a public, or those who act for it, decide—or, it may be, fail to decide—what is to be done. It follows, then, that anyone interested in the problems of the cities ought also to be interested in the way their political systems work.

These systems differ greatly from city to city, and very few have been comprehensively described in print.[1] If one goes to the city hall or public library, one can usually get the principal facts about the legal structure of a city's government—what the elective offices are, how to get on the ballot, how many votes in council are necessary to override the mayor's veto, and the like. But if one cannot do this, it is often not easy to get such simple facts. There is no central place where they are collected for all cities or even for all large ones. And if one wants to go beyond the simple facts to find out how the system "really works," there is often no

---

[1] A notable exception is Wallace Sayre and William Kaufman, *Governing New York City* (New York: Russell Sage Foundation, 1960).

way of getting the information short of going to politicians and others who know and asking them, and this under some circumstances may be practically impossible. Suppose, for example, that one wants to know whether the mayor of a certain city is able to push large undertakings through the city council. One cannot very well call him long distance to ask, and even if one did call him, it would probably be hard to evaluate his answer—if he gave one. Where, then, does one go to get such questions answered?

As an assistance to persons doing research on urban problems, the Joint Center for Urban Studies of the Massachusetts Institute of Technology and Harvard University for several years published in mimeographed form a series of reports on the politics of about twenty-five of the largest cities (excluding New York, Chicago, and a few others) which it distributed to about 200 public libraries, college and university libraries, and research institutes. Some of the reports were much more voluminous than others, but all contained similar information and all were organized in the same way. In most instances the reports were written by graduate students. All the authors supplemented documentary sources with interviews. A considerable number of politicians, newspapermen, civic association professionals, and professors contributed information. Each report was checked for accuracy by three local authorities before its publication.

The chapters that follow are essentially condensations of some of these reports. In each case some additional information has been added (several of the original reports were several years old when the condensations were made) and some changes of interpretation have been made. Therefore the author, while acknowledging his indebtedness to the authors of the reports, takes full responsibility for what appears here. Whereas the purpose of the reports was to provide raw and semi-digested data for the use of research workers, teachers, and students, that of the present volume is to give the general reader a compact, informative account of how certain local political systems work.

The idea is to describe what is normal or typical about the political system of a city. For this reason, what newspa-

permen call "color" and "human interest" has been deliber-
ately excluded. If the mayor is a cigar-chewing Episcopalian,
that fact is not recorded here unless being (or not being) a
cigar-chewing Episcopalian has something to do with the
normal operation of the political system. By the same token,
the personalities and issues that are in the headlines today
are not of interest here except as they exemplify the normal
working of the system, that is, its tendency over time and in
a variety of cases. Most people who write books about politics like to claim that their subjects are topical. Here, the
opposite claim is made; to the extent that it succeeds in its
purpose, this book is *not* topical, or is only incidentally so. It
deals with current events only to reveal the relatively un-
changing features of the various political systems—to use
the phrase loosely, their equilibrium position.

If the reader wonders how anyone can decide what are
and what are not the "normal" features of a political system,
the answer is: by guesswork. The very notion of a political
system involves guesswork. One guesses that by taking account of certain features of the situation and ignoring others one can formulate explanations of what has happened
and predictions of what will happen. If the predictions prove
correct, one assumes that the guesses were good ones. If one
already *knew* precisely what had to be taken into account,
it would be because one already had all the answers, in
which case of course there would have been no need to
construct a theory or to make and test predictions.

The guesswork is not entirely blind, however. There exists
a certain amount of theory, some of it in some sense scien-
tific but most of it hardly more than common sense, that tells
one which features of a situation must be taken into account
(it very rarely tells one just *how* to take them into account,
however) and which can safely be ignored. No one would
doubt, for example, that the presence in a city of large numbers of Negroes is likely to make a difference in its politics.
Nor would one doubt that the number of left-handed people
in the city is of no interest. For an account of the theories on
the basis of which most of the material in this book was
selected, the reader is referred to *City Politics,* a study which
analyzes, along with much other material, the reports that

are here condensed.[2] Incidentally, readers who want explanations of terms like "city charter," "nonpartisanship," and "machine" will find them there.

In order to facilitate comparisons, the material in the following chapters is organized on a common plan. After an introductory paragraph, each chapter begins with a few essential facts about the characteristics of the city's population and economic base. (For convenience in making comparisons, some of these facts are brought together in a table at the end of this introduction, pages 16-17.) The next section describes briefly the formal organization of the city government. But since there is usually a good deal of difference between the way things are "supposed" to be done and the way they actually are done, the next section tells how the formal arrangements are supplemented or modified by informal ones. The following section explains how candidates are nominated and elected and how in general the electoral system operates. Then come a few paragraphs about the part that certain interest groups and influentials—business, labor, minority groups, and the press—play in the politics of the city. The last section of each chapter is a brief case study intended to show how the elements of the political system fit together and work. The idea here is to set the system in motion, so to speak, in order to see what sort of policy outcome it will produce.

What can be learned from a comparison of the nine very different political systems described in this book?

One would like to be able to show how particular causes produce particular effects. If one could trace out *several* links in a causal sequence, that would be especially satisfying. Thus, one might begin by showing how certain "starting place" characteristics of a city, such as its size, rate of growth, economic function, rate of home ownership, or the class or ethnic composition of its population exert a causal influence on the form and style of its government. (By "form and style" is meant whether the electoral system is partisan or nonpartisan, whether the office of mayor is

[2] Edward C. Banfield and James Q. Wilson, *City Politics* (Cambridge, Mass.: Harvard University Press, 1963).

strong or weak, whether the city council is elected on a ward basis or at large, whether the system is centralized or decentralized, and so on.) A second link might be established by showing the causal connections between form and style on the one hand and the content of the city government's policy on the other hand. What difference does it make in terms of the substance of policy that the city elects its mayor on a nonpartisan basis? Do city governments headed by nonpartisan mayors undertake more or less (of what sorts of things?) than city governments headed by partisan ones? Are nonpartisan governments more or less prone to serve special interests (which ones?), and are they more or less prone to corruption or inefficiency? A third link might be established by showing a causal connection between the content of city government policy and the quality of life in the city. One would like to know, for example, whether having an enterprising city government makes the city grow faster, leads to better race relations, or raises the general standard of living.

The reader who tries to formulate general statements along these lines will be tantalized by what he finds in the chapters that follow. He will find some cause-and-effect relations that clearly hold for one or two cities. But when he looks for the same effects from what appear to be the same causes in other cities he is likely to be disappointed.

The difficulty of generalizing along the lines that have just been suggested becomes apparent as soon as one tries to relate "starting place" characteristics—for example, the class character of the city—to the form and structure of government. Philadelphia and St. Louis, two cities with relatively small proportions of white-collar employees and (by non-Southern standards) large proportions of low-income families, have partisan electoral systems and the mayors of both cities are to a considerable extent dependent upon the cooperation of machine bosses. Can we conclude that other cities with similarly constituted populations will have governments that exhibit about the same form and structure? Alas, no. Detroit and Boston, which are much like Philadelphia and St. Louis in the two population characteristics mentioned, both have nonpartisan governments. Detroit, indeed, has long been as much of a "good government" city as Seattle, which has the highest proportion of white-collar employees and the lowest proportion of low-income families of any large city in the United States. It is perhaps not hard to find at least a partial explanation of the anomaly represented by Detroit and Boston: the present form of government is in both cases a heritage that a middle-class elite thrust upon the city before losing power. But why did not the same thing happen in Philadelphia and St. Louis, for these cities also were once ruled by middle-class elites? And why have not Detroit and Boston returned to partisan politics in the years that have elapsed since the middle-class elites lost their power?

Effects that seem to be the same, moreover, may prove to be very different when examined closely. Detroit and Boston, for example, are alike in that they elect their city councils on an at-large basis. But this similarity turns out to be of rather trivial importance, for in Detroit (perhaps because that city is so much larger) a councilman represents a constellation of interest groups, whereas in Boston he is on his own as a "personality." Although formally the same with respect to what one would think could be an important structural feature, the Detroit council plays a different and much more constructive part in the formation of policy than its Boston counterpart.

When one tries to show how the form and style of a city government influence the content of policy the difficulties increase. The task is impossible if one makes the mistake of thinking that what matters most is whether the electoral system is partisan or nonpartisan. All but two of the political systems described in this book are nonpartisan, and the differences in the policies of these seven nonpartisan city governments are in some respects considerable. The structural feature that has the most to do with policy, perhaps, is the degree to which governmental power is centralized. It is not enough that a high degree of centralization be provided by law, however. Miami Metro is an example of a government which, from a purely legal standpoint, is highly centralized; but those who have legal authority do not have much extra-legal influence to go with it, and Metro is therefore more form than substance. As the case of Atlanta shows, one can have a city government which from a purely legal standpoint is rather decentralized, but which is in fact highly centralized through the working of extra-legal arrangements. Or, again, one can have cities where ample legal authority is joined with substantial extra-legal influence, thus producing a centralization that is unusually predictable in its operation. Detroit and Philadelphia are examples. That the mayors of these two cities have great formal *and* informal power is far more important in its effect on policy than that one city is nonpartisan and the other partisan. To see this, one need only compare the range and character of the city government undertakings in Detroit and Philadelphia with those in two other cities (both nonpartisan) whose mayors conspicuously lack both formal and informal power, Los Angeles and Seattle.

It would be nice if we could take the per capita level of general expenditure in a city as a measure of the city government's willingness and ability to get things done. On that basis Boston would have by far the most effective government of any large city in the United States. Unfortunately, the expenditure figures cannot be used in this way. For one thing, it is not at all clear that they measure even approximately the same thing from city to city. (A function that gets state aid in one city may not get it in another, for example.) But even if they did measure the same thing, it would not follow that a high level of expenditure would reflect "effectiveness" in a city government. It might represent that, of course. But it might also represent waste. (Perhaps Boston's level of expenditure is high mainly because Mayor Collins has not been able to eliminate all of the payrollers who were given jobs by Mayor Curley.) Or, again, the level of expenditure might be low because the problems a city has to cope with are relatively simple (it costs less to provide fire protection for new brick buildings than for old wooden ones, for example) or because the income and tastes of the citizens favor a low level. This may explain why Atlanta, a city with a strong mayor, has such a low level of expenditure; it does not *necessarily* explain it, however, for the level of expenditure in Seattle, the city with the highest

median per capita income, is not very much greater than
that of Atlanta.

It is tempting to suggest that the cities with the strong
and enterprising governments are the ones in which newspapers and businessmen's associations play influential parts.
Newspapers and businessmen are, after all, notoriously in
favor of "progress" and "civic improvement," especially when
it is the ordinary taxpayer who will foot the bill, and it
is not hard to find instances where such connections are
visible and direct: the *Miami Herald,* for example, is and
always has been a main support of Metro. But look at Boston. Mayor Collins' administration is strong and enterprising, but the press and business play a very minor part in
Boston's affairs. And look at Los Angeles. The *Los Angeles
Times* and the Chamber of Commerce have long been powerful forces in city politics, but the government of the city is
as weak as they come.

The link between the content of policy and the quality of
life in the city is the hardest of all to demonstrate. The
differences from one big central city to another in the matters that one would expect to be affected by what a city
government does or fails to do turn out upon examination
to be rather minor. As one can see from the table following
this introduction, the rental price of housing, the percentage
of dilapidated housing, and the median years of schooling of
the population vary from city to city within a rather narrow
range. (If the reader does not consider the range narrow, he
should make the same comparisons between central cities
and their suburban rings. He would find that there is more
difference between almost any central city and its suburbs
than between almost any two central cities, even ones as
differently situated as Atlanta and Seattle.) Such differences
as exist, moreover, are to be explained by other causes than
the policies of the city governments. Thus the slightly
higher percentage of dilapidated dwellings in Boston may
be due to the age of the city, and the still higher percentage
in Atlanta and El Paso may be due to the presence of low-
income Negroes and Mexicans. The difference in median
years of schooling may reflect the presence in some cities of
large numbers of migrants from the rural South and in

others (Seattle and Los Angeles, for example) an unusual growth of space-age industry. From very different starting places (economically, culturally, and otherwise), the large central cities seem to come to very similar outcomes. And this in spite of differences in the form and style of their governments and in the content of their policies.

In the search for differences that can be explained causally we are apt to overlook similarities, some of which may be of greater importance than the differences. From the nine accounts that follow, several striking similarities meet the eye. For one thing, all nine of the city governments are honestly and ably run. To be sure, they are far from perfect. But if Lincoln Steffens were alive today, he could not possibly write a book like *The Shame of the Cities* about them or for that matter about any other large American cities. Such corruption as there is today extends, so to say, from the bottom up and not, as in Steffens' day, from the top down. Today there is no big city notorious for its bad government; what is said about Boston in the chapter that follows—that no man suspected of being a rascal has any chance of being elected mayor—could be said of any big city. Nowadays incompetence and corruption in high places is probably more prevalent in state than in city government. Almost all the recent mayors of the nine cities described here have been competent at the very least, and of those in office when this was written (June, 1964) at least four—Allen of Atlanta, Collins of Boston, Cavanagh of Detroit, and Tucker of St. Louis—were outstanding figures. (If the powers of his office gave him more scope, perhaps Yorty of Los Angeles would also belong on this list.) Since city politics is rarely a route to high state and national office, the wonder is that so many men of first-rate ability devote themselves to it.

Another similarity—and a rather surprising one—is that the quality of city government has been improving despite the departure of the "good government"-minded middle class for the suburbs and its replacement by Negro and Southern white migrants who, because of the backwardness of the rural places they come from, are in general far from civic-minded. One would expect that as the lower-class tide rises in the central cities the governments of these cities would get worse. Perhaps they will when it has risen far enough. But, as several notable examples—St. Louis, Boston, and Philadelphia, among others—show, so far at least the quality of government has been getting better, not worse.

Another striking similarity in the politics of the cities is their conservatism. No American city elects radicals to local office or experiments with unorthodox schemes. (Milwaukee had a Socialist mayor for some time, but in practice his socialism was simply businesslike administration.) What is more, none, or practically none, supports municipal services at a level comparable to that generally expected of the federal government. Almost everywhere city parks, schools, libraries, and police forces leave much to be desired; even so, city governments have to struggle hard to find the revenue to support them. The big urban renewal projects and other public works are almost always for business-serving purposes, such as to dislodge "undesirables" from areas adjacent to the downtown business district and replace them with "good customers." In most of the chapters that follow it is asserted that newspapers and organized businessmen have a great deal of political influence and that labor and minority groups have little. It would be a mistake to conclude, however, that city governments are conservative because the man on the street is somehow excluded from political participation. The fact is that the man on the street is himself conservative in local affairs; often he is so even when he is very liberal in state and national affairs. (The reason for this may be that he knows that his property tax will go up if city expenditures go up, whereas the cost of state and federal largesse always seems to fall mainly on someone else.) Not only does he put conservatives, or at the most moderates, in office, but he checks them afterward when they propose bond issues for public improvements. Thus Seattle, with the highest median per capita income of any large city in the country, supports its government meagerly and on a hand-to-mouth basis. By and large, however, the middle class is more generous with public expenditures than the homeowning working class: Atlanta, the city with the business "power structure," and Detroit, the city with the powerful left-wing labor union, are instructive examples; in both cities working-class homeowners are the obstacle in the way of ambitious plans for civic improvement. Finally, look at Los Angeles, where the man on the street insists both that the city trim his palm trees and that it leave his water unfluoridated.

Another feature that the big city political systems have in common is a remarkable ability to manage and contain the conflicts, some of them very bitter and deep-seated, that are so conspicuous a feature of the polyglot metropolis. Detroit, where workers and management, radicals and conservatives, and Negroes and anti-Negroes stand eyeball to eyeball, is a good example; Atlanta is another. These differ from the other big cities only in degree. Although tensions everywhere are great, there has not been any outbreak of mass violence in any large city for many years. The civil rights demonstrations of the last couple of years, far from constituting exceptions to this proposition, are evidence in support of it, for although they have thrown off many sparks, none of the demonstrations has started a conflagration. In city after city—Atlanta, Detroit, St. Louis, and Philadelphia are notable examples—local politicians are laboring energetically and with a considerable degree of success to lighten the heavy weight of injustice that holds the Negro down. In some cities—Los Angeles and Detroit, for example—the white "power structure" has helped the Negro community get representation on the city council and in other elective offices.

Finally, the political systems of the big cities—not only the nine described here, but the others as well—are alike in this: they do not give rise to or nourish anti-democratic extremist movements. One would think that rabble-rousers might make their way to national attention by being elected mayor of Atlanta, Detroit, or Los Angeles. Thanks to television, the techniques of demagoguery do indeed work remarkably well in those cities. But strangely enough the demagogues, once they get themselves into office, turn into conscientious and responsible administrators. Even when they are trying to get elected for the first time, they campaign against "professional politicians," "the power structure," and other figments of the voters' imaginations and not, as they might, against Negroes.

To be sure, in Seattle a right-wing organization helped defeat two candidates for the city council in 1964 by circulating a broadsheet charging them with being members of the board of directors of the American Civil Liberties Union. But this sort of thing is very rare in American city politics. In general the local political systems are nearly impervious to ideology.

No doubt many factors account for these similarities among the political systems of the big cities. The presence of large numbers of professionals whose tenure is made secure by merit systems probably accounts to a large extent for the greater honesty and competence of the city governments, for example. Even if he were inclined to play fast and loose, a mayor would find it hard to do so now that many of his chief subordinates are career civil servants, not politicians.

Another factor which may account for some of these similarities is the separation which in most—but not all—cases exists between the local political system on the one hand and the state and national systems on the other. In the case of the nonpartisan cities, this separation is established (not always very effectively, to be sure) in law. In other cases a considerable degree of separation may result from informal arrangements. Mayor Tucker of St. Louis, for example, was in the Democratic party but not of it. The reform mayors of Philadelphia, Clark and Dilworth, although Democrats, occupied a different sphere from the party bosses; both of these mayors were called "independents," but they could as well have been called "nonpartisans." However it comes about, separation between local and state and national politics must tend to discourage those politicians who are after the largest prizes from seeking office in the city. This in turn must greatly reduce the incentive that exists to inject ideological issues into local politics, and it must also increase somewhat the likelihood that the mayor will be a man—like Allen of Atlanta, Tucker of St. Louis, or Clinton of Seattle—whose motive in running for office is to serve his city.

Surely, however, the principal factor working to produce

these similarities is the structure of the electoral process it-self. Where only two candidates oppose each other (and this is the case in a run-off, as distinguished from a prelimi-nary, mayoralty election) the logic of the situation compels them to take positions calculated to attract at least 51 per cent of the vote. Given the distribution of interests and opinions that exists in a large American city, this excludes extremists of all kinds and it gives a decided advantage to those candidates—necessarily moderates—who can attract strong support from diverse sectors of the electorate. The mayor of Atlanta is a case in point. So long as he has the solid support of the business-led middle class *and* the Ne-groes he is unbeatable. And he is likely to have this support because neither the middle class nor the Negroes can elect a man who will be theirs and theirs alone. In the preliminary election such a man might win, but in the run-off he would surely lose. The necessity of creating voting alliances often gives more weight to minorities—not only to Negroes, but to homeowners, tax-savers, "good government" and reform enthusiasts, and others—than their numbers in the popula-tion would justify, for the politician in a two-candidate sys-tem will "pay" the most for the marginal votes that will bring him victory, and these votes are most often to be found in such minorities. Thus the structure of the political sys-tems tends to create coalitions of moderates. In this, as in much else, the political systems of the cities reflect the genius of American politics generally.

Selected Comparative Data

	Atlanta	Boston	Dade County (Miami)
Population, 1960 (*in thousands*)	487	697	935
% of change in population, 1950-60	47	—13	89
% foreign stock[1]	3	45	28
% non-white	38	10	15
% in white collar jobs	44	44	46
Median years of schooling	10.5	11.2	11.4
Median family income	$5029	$5747	$5348
% of family income under $3,000	27	17	23
% of family income over $10,000	16	14	14
% of dwelling units owner-occupied	46	27	59
% of dwelling units dilapidated	7.5	3.9	2.1
Median gross rent (*per month*)	$65	$78	$85
Per capita general municipal expenditure[2]	$85	$243	$101[3]

[1] I.e. foreign-born persons plus native population of foreign or mixed parentage.
[2] Total general expenditures, less education, for the fiscal year 1961.
Source: Municipal Yearbook, 1963.

on the Cities in this Volume*

Detroit	El Paso	Los Angeles	Phila-delphia	St. Louis	Seattle
1670	277	2479	2003	750	557
—10	112	26	—3	—13	19
32	40	33	29	14	31
29	3	17	27	29	8
40	49	50	41	38	55
10.0	11.1	12.1	9.6	8.8	12.2
$6069	$5211	$6896	$5782	$5355	$6942
19	22	14	17	22	12
18	13	25	14	11	23
58	58	46	62	38	57
2.6	6.6	1.4	2.0	4.4	2.3
$77	$61	$78	$65	$66	$75
$135	$68	$102	$137	$118	$92

[3] Miami only; Dade County not available.
* Source: 1960 Census of Population and 1960 Housing Census.

ATLANTA:

Strange Bedfellows

Atlanta has been described as a city in which a small "power elite" of big businessmen and manufacturers makes all important decisions in public matters, leaving their execution to an "understructure" of elected and appointed officials and lesser businessmen.[1] Whatever may have been the situation when this description was made, it is different now. Atlanta is governed by politicians with the help of the press and an alliance between two voting blocs—one of businessmen and middle-class whites who are interested in "good government" and "civic progress," and the other of Negroes aiming to free themselves of the disabilities that have so long held them down. To be sure, the principal politician is a big businessman, the white middle class takes its cues from the business community (as do many of the Negroes), and the city government's policies for the most part are business-serving. (When a former mayor said Atlanta was "too busy to hate," he meant that the businessmen had decided that fighting desegregation would be bad for business.) Nevertheless the city is run by voters and politicians, not by a "power elite."

Population and Economy

Atlanta's population increased by 47 per cent to 487,000 between 1950 and 1960. The increase was almost entirely due to annexation of parts of Fulton County. In 1950 the area of the city was just under 37 square miles; ten years later it was 127 square miles. The metropolitan area includes five counties and has a population of more than 1,000,000, about one-quarter of the population of the state.

[1] Floyd Hunter, *Community Power Structure* (Chapel Hill: University of North Carolina Press, 1953).

Negroes constituted 38 per cent of the city's population in 1960. The Negro population is increasing faster than the white in the city (elsewhere in the metropolitan area it is the other way around); most of the increase is occurring in the old, central section. Aside from the Negroes, there is no numerically important ethnic or nationality group. There were 16,116 persons of foreign stock in 1960, and about 15,000 Jews. White Protestant church members outnumber Catholics 19 to 1 in Fulton County. Being a Baptist, while not indispensable to political success, is very helpful.

The northwest and to a lesser extent the northeast sections of the city are occupied by a prosperous white middle class. Lower middle- and working-class whites live in the southeast section; many of these people are poor "crackers" who have been pushed off small farms since World War II, and are in closer touch with the Klu Klux Klan than with the city's leadership. The southwest section has a growing middle class. The Negro population is clustered largely about the central city but has pierced eastern, southern, and northwestern sectors.

In the last twenty-five years Atlanta has become the commercial, industrial, and administrative capital of the Southeast. Long a center of transportation and commerce, it is now a manufacturing center also. In recent years many small and some middle-sized industries have moved into the metropolitan area. New industrial parks have opened, and existing industries, including Lockheed Aircraft, the state's largest employer, have made significant expansions. Job opportunities have been increasing faster than population for some time. Some of the city's largest industries are controlled from the Northeast. Atlanta is also a branch-office city and the regional headquarters of a great many government agencies.

How the Government Is Organized

The city has the weak-mayor-council form of government. The mayor is elected for a four-year term and receives a salary of $20,000. A vice-mayor and president of the board of aldermen and sixteen aldermen (two from each ward) are elected at large for four-year terms. The vice-mayor is paid $5,400 and $1,200 in expense money annually. Aldermen are paid $3,600 in salary and $1,200 in expense money.

The board of aldermen approves the budget, appropriates all funds, passes on zoning matters, issues alcoholic beverage licenses, levies taxes, and exercises legislative control of the city's thirty-three departments. In theory it may enact ordinances wherever these do not conflict with state laws, but since the Georgia General Assembly is given to legislating on the affairs of the city, this does not amount to home rule. (In 1953 the legislature, over aldermanic protests, completely revamped the city's governing body, replacing a twenty-seven-member bicameral council with the present unicameral one.) The board's tax powers are sharply limited; it may not enact sales, payroll, or certain other taxes; accordingly, its main reliance is upon property taxes.

The board operates on the committee system, each committee having legislative direction of a particular city department. However, the mayor appoints the committees and names their chairmen. He is a member *ex officio* of all committees and may therefore appear before any of them whenever he likes. (He may appear before the full board only by unanimous consent, however.) He has a veto which the board may override by a two-thirds vote.

The mayor himself appoints only his administrative assistant, a $17,500 executive whose duties generally compare with those of a city manager, and his executive secretary. His appointments of members to the many official boards and citizens advisory committees are subject to ratification by aldermen, but the ratification in practice is largely a formality. He appoints judges of municipal courts from a list of nominees drawn up by an advisory body; these appointments are also subject to aldermanic ratification.

Most city department heads are *nominated* by the mayor and then elected by the board of aldermen. The law says aldermen need not accept a mayor's nominee, but it forbids nominations from the floor. There has never been a test of what would happen if the aldermen were to reject a mayor's nominee.

Most city department heads are subject to reelection every four years. Exceptions are the police and fire chiefs and the traffic engineer, who are elected to indefinite terms on good behavior, and the library and personnel directors, who serve at the pleasure of their departmental advisory boards. In practice, however, all department heads enjoy secure tenure. Their terms have been fixed to span any change of administration; a new mayor hostile to his predecessor's regime would find it very difficult to "clean house."

The budget is fixed each January by the finance committee after a budget commission has estimated the revenue for the new year. The budget commission includes the mayor, the city comptroller, the chairman of the aldermanic finance committee, and two aldermen elected by their colleagues.

SCHOOLS

The board of education is independent of the city government, except that it must depend upon it for the levying of taxes. It consists of nine members (one from each ward and one at large) elected on a nonpartisan basis for four-year terms. Its president is paid $3,600 a year and is elected by other members of the board. The pay of other members is $3,000 a year. They include one woman and one Negro.

THE COUNTY GOVERNMENT

Eight per cent of Atlanta's population lives in DeKalb County; the rest lives in Fulton. Each county government is run by three commissioners elected at large on a partisan basis. Because the bulk of Fulton County voters live in Atlanta, its commissioners are almost invariably Atlantans. For the same reason, the commissioners are oriented to the downtown business community and are sensitive to the Negro vote, though in lesser degree than are the elected city officials.

Commissioners serve four-year terms. Their salaries are $5,000 a year, supplemented by $75 monthly expense allowances. In effect the commissioners are elected in the Democratic primaries; no Republican has sought county elective office in modern times.

The Fulton County government clearly is overshadowed

by the Atlanta city government. City supremacy was established in 1952 with the enactment of a legislative package called the Plan of Improvement. Functions of the city and county governments, which had been overlapping, were then unscrambled. The county was left mainly with traditional county government functions: the courts, health, education, and welfare. It retained power to build roads, accomplish zoning, fix speed laws, issue business licenses, and so on, in unincorporated areas. But otherwise it was required to contract with the City of Atlanta for fire and police protection, for water and sewage, and for garbage collection and library services in unincorporated areas. The city and county maintain a joint planning (zoning) board, and a combined tax assessing and tax collection organization. (The governing authorities of each pass finally on zoning matters and levy taxes.)

Fulton County has a county manager who is paid a base salary of $16,000 a year. He appoints all administrative department heads except the county attorney, the clerk to the commissioners, and the voting registrar, who are appointed by the commissioners. In fact, but not in law, his appointments are made with approval of commissioners. Judges, the clerk of court, the county ordinary, the sheriff, the coroner, and the surveyor are elective officers.

How It Really Works

Atlanta mayors (there have been only two since 1942) are not as weak as these legal-formal arrangements might suggest. They have very little patronage at their disposal. "I could build the stadium where it ought to be if I had some jobs to give out," Mayor Ivan Allen, Jr. told a visitor early in 1964. But he added, "I don't favor a patronage system, however; civil service produces better men." In practice as well as in theory, a mayor may influence the direction of legislation by nominating strong men as department heads. In general, however, he has his way with the aldermen mainly through the force of persuasion and by marshalling community support, especially that of the press, behind him.

In controversial matters aldermen are usually willing to

let the mayor assume leadership and, of course, run any political risks. Many people in Atlanta think that the board is altogether too weak.

In the making of the budget, however, the chairman of the finance committee exercises a good deal of independent power. He and the comptroller do most of the planning. Meetings of the full committee are held only when the budget is up for final adoption, or when major appropriations are to be discussed. The recommendations of the chairman are seldom seriously challenged. However, the mayor, an *ex officio* member of the committee, exerts a strong influence on city spending.

Strong committee chairmen not infrequently dominate departments and function less as legislators than as administrators. But the committee system does not prevent a mayor from achieving an excellent working relationship with department heads. Former Mayor William B. Hartsfield, who served for twenty-three years, commanded not only the administrative loyalties of the department heads but their political loyalty as well. In his campaigns he could count on their help in seeing that employees in their departments voted, and voted the right way. He could also count on them to help influence the general public. As a rule the candidates who opposed Hartsfield sought to woo certain key department heads away from him. The police chief, an astute politician, was a chief objective in such efforts. But department heads seem to have remained loyal to Hartsfield. The election of 1961, in which Hartsfield did not seek re-election, saw a change. That year department heads kept discreetly out of the mayoralty race. Whether they will do so again remains to be seen.

The mayor's power, someone said, is like a three-legged stool. The press is one leg. The business "power structure," together with the "good government"-minded middle class that takes its lead from the "power structure," is another. The third leg is the Negro community. It was Mayor Hartsfield who brought the three legs together and made them into a stool. When he first took office, depression, graft, and incompetence had left the city government in bad financial straits. He instituted businesslike fiscal practices, found a way to finance operating costs from current revenues, and inspired such confidence in the business community that the local bankers bailed the city out. Hartsfield's standing thereafter was so high that the relative weakness of his office made no difference. Although not a liberal on race matters, he saw very early that a "good government" regime needed a heavy Negro vote in order to stay in office, and he responded realistically. "You gave me 1,500 votes and I slipped into office," he is supposed to have told Negro leaders after his first election. "Get me 15,000 votes and I won't have to slip in." In 1957 he got nine-tenths of more than 20,000 Negro votes. By this time, however, he was widely disliked in the white working-class districts of the southeast and west sides and was being criticized by the press. To save him and the coalition he had put together, leaders of the business community are said to have persuaded the newspapers to endorse him for reelection, something they had not planned to do.

Although he does not have the authority that long and successful service gave Hartsfield, Mayor Allen, who was elected in 1961, has managed to keep the three-legged stool under himself.

How They Get Elected

All city officials are elected in a series of three nonpartisan elections. A primary is held in September of every fourth year (1961, 1965, etc.). This is followed by a "runover" two weeks later in which the voters choose between the two top candidates for each position (if any receives a majority in the primary no runover is necessary); the candidates thus "nominated" run for a third time in a general election in December.

This three-election system is under attack. Opponents say that the third election is unnecessary and may work an injustice because a light vote then could upset a heavy vote in the primary. In 1963 an election study commission recommended changing the state law to have one nonpartisan election followed by a runover for any contests in which a candidate fails to secure a majority the first time.

Georgia law provides that any political party or organization nominating candidates for office in a primary must also elect an executive committee of the party organization. Until 1953 the City Democratic Executive Committee attested the qualifications of all candidates for local office. In that year a Negro educator sought to qualify as a candidate for the city board of education and the committee refused to put his name on the ballot. A court ordered him qualified, however, and he was elected at large. After this the personnel of the committee was changed and "Democratic" was dropped from its name. It has since qualified all candidates who met the legal requirements.

THE 1961 MAYORALTY ELECTION

When Mayor Hartsfield announced, in June 1961, that he would not run again, the business-led coalition had already made preparations to elect his successor. Its candidate, Ivan Allen, Jr., was a wealthy businessman (his office-equipment supply firm had sales of $8,000,000 in 1961) and the son of a distinguished civic leader. Allen had run for governor a few years before and was currently president of the Atlanta Chamber of Commerce. He was known as a conservative (running for governor he had favored the county unit system, which gave the rural "rednecks" control of the state) and as an honest, energetic, and capable administrator. It is doubtful whether he was the choice of the entire "power structure," however; some leading businessmen at first declined to support him on the grounds that a businessman could not possibly be elected.

Allen's plan of campaign organization was ready the day Hartsfield announced his retirement. He appointed a ward chief in each ward and sixty precinct chairmen. These in turn recruited volunteers—2,337 of them, as it turned out—to make telephone calls on his behalf. Campaign headquarters supplied each volunteer with a kit containing buttons, stickers, campaign cards, a letter of appreciation from the candidate, and, most important, 100 listings cut from the telephone book. The workers were given suggestions about how to make the phone calls and how to respond to questions that might be asked; work sheets and return envelopes were supplied to encourage quick reporting of results. Allen also sent to all registered voters a letter, with an enclosed reply card, asking what the voter thought was the most important issue of the campaign.

Allen went to fish-fries, Kiwanis luncheons, and rallies—as many as five a night—and he used a good deal of paid political time on television. His three sons helped him with young people, many of whom were too young to vote but whose enthusiasm seemed to be contagious. His campaign was based on a carefully worked out strategy. He had employed a professional analyst to study the returns of the previous election and to do some polling. From the analyst's reports he knew that if he got a heavy vote in the middle-class districts of the north side and from the Negroes he was bound to win. Expecting that there would be a runover election, he hoped that the man he faced in it (there were four other candidates in the primary) would be the one easiest for him to beat. To help bring this about he picked as his chief target an arch-segregationist who had run against Hartsfield in 1957. At the first rally, Allen dramatically pointed his finger at this man and declared that Atlanta was too progressive a city to elect one of his ilk. From then on the contest was between him and the arch-segregationist.

In his effort to get a heavy Negro vote, Allen depended heavily upon the Atlanta Negro Voters League, which had been formed in 1948 when there was danger that the revival of the Republican party might split the Negroes. It had two sets of officers, one Democratic and the other Republican, and it endorsed a slate on a nonpartisan basis. It maintained a block-by-block organization in the Negro precincts, sponsoring meetings at churches and larger mass meetings at which favored candidates were invited to speak and to answer questions. Early in the morning of election day it distributed flyers listing its approved slate throughout the Negro community.

Allen did not need to "buy" the League's support. Negroes were accustomed to bloc voting for the least objectionable candidate, and Allen had established himself as that. The League had no real alternative but to support him. He and his business associates may, however (there is no way of knowing), have thrown some business to the Negro leaders, not to get their support but to provide them the wherewithal to get out a heavy vote.

By election day the Allen volunteers had made 102,983 telephone calls. This was about half as many as had been called for by the original campaign plan, but it was enough. Allen was the high man with 38,000 votes. The other four candidates split 62,000. As Allen had hoped, the arch-segregationist came in second. In the runover, Allen won by nearly 30,000 votes in a record turn-out of more than 100,-000. He got a fraction of 1 per cent less than a majority of the white vote. But he got practically all the Negro vote.

Allen's campaign cost at least $200,000. He was rich enough to afford it, but he undoubtedly got substantial help from his business friends.

ALDERMANIC RACES

Aldermanic races are overshadowed by mayoralty contests. Rarely does a particular race assume importance. The tendency therefore is for incumbents to prevail; one alderman has served forty-two years, another thirty-six, one more than twenty, and several more than ten. Turnover on the board often occurs through the retirement or death of incumbents. When a vacancy occurs, the board fills it by electing a man nominated by the ward colleague of the departing alderman. Such "ward courtesy" appointees enjoy a decided advantage when they seek reelection. Five vacancies occurred on the board between 1962 and mid-1964. Two involved the same seat; hence there were four appointees on the board, one being the appointee of an appointee.

If he has serious opposition, a candidate for alderman may spend as much as $10,000 to $30,000 on his campaign. The election being at large, most of the money goes for television time. Some candidates undoubtedly get substantial help from downtown businessmen; liquor interests are said to be financial supporters of several. The "power structure," however, has little or no interest in aldermanic races.

Few aldermanic seats go uncontested. Incumbents, however, rarely face more than one opponent, for two reasons. Election being by majority vote, the idea is prevalent that

if more than one candidate opposes an incumbent the opposition vote will be split and the incumbent will win. Also,
because elections are at large, candidates must be favorably
known beyond the bounds of their own wards. This is an
especial handicap for Negro candidates, who must muster
both a substantial white vote and a solid Negro vote. So far
no Negro candidate has been successful.

As constituted in 1964, the board included no Negroes,
no women, and no representatives of labor. Its president was
a hard-working, civic-minded young Jewish real estate man
who was thought of as a possible successor to Mayor Allen.
Although he was not wealthy, this man spent 90 per cent of
his time on public business. The others on the board represented a variety of occupations: there were three lawyers,
two insurance men, a salesman, a dairy products executive, a
banker, an oil company executive, an athletic coach, a chem-
ical company executive, a retired engineer, a grocer, a builder,
and the owner of a barber supply company. None was a
member of the city's business elite, although the banker, a
vice-president of one of the more politically-minded banks,
was oriented in that direction. Two of the aldermen were
Republicans, elected in 1961, the first of their party to hold
office in modern city history. They work together, but there
is nothing partisan about their activities.

THE OUTLOOK FOR THE COALITION

The future strength of the Negro–middle-class-white voting
alliance will depend largely upon three factors: (1) the
number of Negroes and middle-class whites who are in the
electorate and who turn out to vote, (2) the extent to
which each group votes as a bloc, and (3) the ability of the
two groups to agree upon the same candidates. With regard
to the first two of these factors at least, the outlook is somewhat mixed.

Middle-class whites have been moving out of Atlanta as
they have out of other cities. The city, however, has pursued
them with annexations, and it will probably continue to do
so. Working-class white districts will not be annexed except
where such a move is unavoidable. Negro leaders favor annexations in the fear that otherwise they (the Negroes)

may constitute a majority—a situation which they know would be unworkable. Although the number (and percentage) of Negroes in the city has been increasing for many years, the long-term trend may change and so upset the present balance; impatience at the South's slow rate of change may lead to a mass exodus of Negroes to Northern cities. Also, the number of "rednecks" moving to the city from submarginal farms is large and increasing; in the next twenty years "rednecks" may replace Negroes as Atlanta's working class.

Working-class whites in Atlanta are less inclined to vote than are Negroes. (About 75 per cent of the eligible Negroes are registered; among whites, middle class *and* working class, the comparable figure is 65 per cent.) The authorities are therefore taking unusual steps to encourage registration. The 1958 Georgia Voter Registration Act provided elaborate qualification procedures, including a literacy test, in order to make it hard for Negroes to vote. But in Fulton County these procedures are not used to serve the purpose for which they were intended; on the contrary, every effort is made to increase Negro registration. Registration units have been set up on a neighborhood basis, sometimes in schoolhouses, and there is talk of sending mobile units from street to street.

It is by no means certain that either the Negroes or the middle-class whites will continue to vote as a bloc. One danger is that the growth of the Republican party may split the vote of both groups along party lines. It was partly to prevent this that Mayor Hartsfield had the word "Democratic" taken out of the name of the City Executive Committee back in 1953. But Republican strength has been growing in the upper-middle-class north side; two Republicans were elected (although not under party label, of course) to the board of aldermen in 1961, and one went to the state senate from an Atlanta district the following year. There is also some talk of having Republican primary elections. Such a development would cut a large part of the white middle class off from the coalition.

There is less danger that the rise of the Republican party will reduce bloc voting among the Negroes. In that quarter the real danger is that the Negro Voters League will be discredited by the militant wing of the civil rights movement and will cease to be able to deliver votes as it has in the past. In 1964 there were many who said that the Negro vote was no longer for sale. If this is so—and it remains to be seen—the Negro vote may be relatively small and scattered.

If Negroes and middle-class whites continue to vote as blocs, they are likely to vote for—and almost certain to vote *against*—the same candidates. Like the "power structure" itself, middle-class whites tend to think that, like it or not, Atlanta must come to terms with the Negro if it is to continue to grow and prosper; they will therefore support Mayor Allen's kind of liberalism and oppose any arch-segregationist. Even those who are less than liberal on race matters will support Allen because the alternative, an arch-segregationist, is almost sure to lack his "good government" orientation. Negroes, too, if they vote in a bloc, will have to vote for Allen or for someone like him even if they find his record disappointing (Hartsfield gave the Negro practically nothing in return for his vote), because he will be the least unattractive alternative. Something Mayor Allen recently said about businessmen could apply as well to both the white middle class and the Negro. "The businessman," the mayor said, "is trained to make a rational decision. Knowing that I have the ability to be elected, the businessman is going to support me whether he agrees with my views on race relations or not."

Interest Groups and Influentials

BUSINESS

There is no doubt that Atlanta has an informal, business-led "power structure" that is of considerable importance in city affairs. The heads of the three principal department stores, the three or four biggest real estate firms, the utilities, manufacturing companies, and major banks undoubtedly take more than a normal amount of interest in matters affecting the area's growth and prosperity. It would be easy to exaggerate the range of matters on which a "top power elite" "sets the line on policy," however. Frequently the principal business leaders cannot agree among themselves. (Between two of the principal banks, the First National and the Citizens and Southern, a feud exists which has jeopardized many worthy causes; people speak of "The War of the Banks.") Even when they agree, the business leaders do not always get their way. Mayor Allen and his predecessor have both taken positions the business community did not approve.

On the race issue most of the big businessmen are personally far from liberal. However, they have been persuaded by the newspapers and the politicians that desegregation is inevitable and efforts to delay it will only harm the city's "image." When Mayor Allen returned to Atlanta after testifying in favor of the federal civil rights bill, he found that his fellow businessmen all opposed the stand he had taken. They were so "hot after my skin," he said afterward, that he got Ralph McGill of the *Constitution* to talk to some of them. Later the Chamber of Commerce's magazine, reporting on the mayor's trip to Washington, said, "Certainly the Forward Atlanta advertising kitty [a fund raised by the chamber to boost the city] couldn't have bought the round of praise Allen earned for Atlanta, from Congress to the editorial pages of the *New York Times*. The wire services built it into the biggest Atlanta-image impact since the city peacefully desegregated its schools."

The man generally supposed to be at the very top of the "power structure" is Robert W. Woodruff, head of the Coca Cola Company and of the Trust Company of Georgia, one of the city's largest banks. Woodruff is rarely in Atlanta ("He couldn't find his way around town, he comes here so seldom"), but his presence is felt nonetheless. His was the only picture on Mayor Hartsfield's office wall, and Mayor Allen is known to have a high regard for him. Many people doubt, however, that he takes much part in Atlanta's affairs; along with the rest of the "power structure," he may have more and bigger fish to fry at the state capital.

Three associations of businessmen, the leadership of which overlaps greatly, play important parts in civic affairs.

The Chamber of Commerce launches ideas which are often taken up as official city policy, and it is always much involved in efforts to get bond issues approved. The Central Atlanta Association is particularly concerned with the downtown business district and has taken the lead in efforts to improve expressways, mass transit, and urban renewal. Its weekly newsletter is widely read and respected. The Uptown Association is a vehicle used by banks and other property owners to maintain a boundary line against expansion of the Negro district. To achieve this purpose it supports nonresidential urban renewal projects.

LABOR

The Atlanta Labor Council, AFL-CIO, represents 96 locals claiming 41,000 members. Its leadership is politically aggressive. It promotes voter registration (it has a full-time worker for this, and claims to have increased the rate of registration among its members from 14 to 38 per cent) and carries on political education. A screening committee gathers information about candidates and presents it to delegates, who then endorse a slate. Although labor endorsements are actively sought by candidates, they are not worth much. Union members rarely vote as a bloc; most of them ignore the endorsements made by the delegates.

The bulk of the Atlanta blue collar workers are rural in background, which is to say that they are racially prejudiced and vote segregationist. The labor leaders in the city, however, are on the moderate side; in the civil rights struggle within the city they have spoken out for "law and order." The leaders' position on this issue does not seem to have weakened their standing with their members; on the other hand, it does not seem to have influenced the members either.

THE PRESS

The city's two principal newspapers have been under a single nonresident ownership since 1950. The morning *Atlanta Constitution* (circ. 202,642), the evening *Atlanta Journal* (circ. 254,622), and the Sunday *Journal and Constitution* (circ. 504,761) are part of the Cox chain. They have separate publishers (the publisher of the *Constitution* is Ralph McGill, the syndicated columnist), editors, and reportorial staffs, and there is some difference, although rarely a sharp one, in their stands on local affairs. The *Constitution* is the more liberal: in January, 1964, it advocated passage of the federal civil rights bill. In general both papers share the views of the business community. But influence seems to run as much or more from them to the "power structure" as the other way around; on the civil rights issue, for example, the newspapers have led the way for years. To rural Georgians, including many members of the state legislature, they typify all that is wrong with the big city. "Them lyin' Atlanta newspapers," the "rednecks" say.

In local politics both papers usually remain neutral until just before the election. Then the big combined Sunday edition endorses candidates in nearly all races, and a barrage of supporting editorials follows in both papers until election day. This support is said to be worth about 5,000 votes in a city-wide election. Several candidates, however, have been elected to the board of aldermen without newspaper support. The papers have strongly backed both Hartsfield and Allen.

A third daily newspaper, the afternoon and Sunday *Atlanta Times,* began publication June 12, 1964. Its publisher is James C. Davis, an arch-segregationist who represented the Atlanta district in Congress for sixteen years until his defeat in 1962. The paper is said to be owned by about 4,500 stockholders, all Georgians, with a number of Atlanta businessmen and professionals on its board of directors. At the end of its first six months, the *Times* did not appear to be doing very well. It claimed a circulation of 100,000 (the *Journal's* circulation dropped about 12,000 during these six months), but its edition ran only 26 pages at the height of the Christmas shopping season (the *Journal* had 56 pages, with more advertising). According to a *New York Times* report (December 12, 1964), the *Atlanta Times* was short of capital and in a management crisis of sorts because of the death of its general manager.

NEGROES

By Southern standards Negroes have long had an unusual
degree of influence in Atlanta affairs. There are several reasons for this, aside from the size and importance of the Negro vote. One is that the city is the home of six Negro
colleges and universities, which have supplied leadership.
Another is that the Negro middle class is large and prosperous. Atlanta has many wealthy Negro business and professional men. They seldom run for office or step into the
limelight, but their money gives them influence with both
Negro and white politicians.

Until a few years ago Negro business and political leaders
who "worked with" white business and political interests
were the only spokesmen for the Negro community whose
views mattered. "Responsible" Negroes, especially "Colonel"
(the title is honorary) A. T. Walden, an aged (he was sev-
enty-eight years old in 1964) retired lawyer and self-styled
"civil consultant," helped Hartsfield and Allen placate the
Negro community and get its vote, and in the process pros-
pered mightily. Recently, however, other younger Negro
leaders have appeared whose connection with the business
community is neither close nor rewarding and who think
Walden and his associates have done little but feather their
own nests through their association with the white "power
structure." These young militants call Walden and his like
"doves" and themselves "hawks." The "hawks" favor direct
action when negotiation proves too slow. They include a
dentist who is head of the 7,000-member branch of the
NAACP, and the local leader of the Student Nonviolent
Coordinating Committee. "If we aren't out there demon-
strating," the SNCC man said, "those people who like to
talk around conference tables won't have anything to talk
about."

There are two Negro newspapers, the *Atlanta Daily
World* and the *Atlanta Inquirer,* a weekly. The *World* (circ.
20,000 daily, 25,000 Sundays), which has sometimes billed
itself as the largest Negro-owned daily in the United States,
is owned by the estate of the late W. A. Scott, a Mississippi
Negro minister and banker who also owned papers in other

Southern cities. It is Republican, and militants accuse it of "Uncle Tomism." The *Inquirer* was started in 1961 by young business and professional people who wanted a more outspoken voice on civil rights. Its first editor was Carl Holman. The paper lost some of its quality but none of its militancy when he left to join the United States Civil Rights Commission.

How Issues Are Handled

The alliance between the business-led white middle class and the Negro is the main fact of local politics and government; only within the limits that it allows can anything be done, and much of what is done is for the purpose of holding it together.

What happens when the alliance fails can be seen from the fate of an $80 million city-county bond proposal that was voted on in the summer of 1962. Mayor Allen campaigned hard for the proposal, which he and the business community thought essential for the development of the city, but it was defeated overwhelmingly. Part of the trouble was timing (the election was held just after the tax bills had been sent out), but mainly it was a break-down of the white-middle-class–Negro alliance. The white middle class voted for the bonds, but most of the Negroes failed to turn out. Either because the Negro Voters League had not been induced by the white business community to go all out or for other reasons, the Negro vote, although favorable to the bonds, was light. Lower-middle-class and working-class whites on the south side of the city turned out in surprising numbers to vote against the bonds, some because they wanted to keep taxes down and others because they had heard a rumor that $5 million offered by an anonymous donor toward the construction of a $9 million cultural center was being put up by a "Yankee" philanthropist. They also felt the cultural center would attract Negroes into a presently all-white residential district. ("Anything anyone is opposed to is tied to the race issue," Allen told an interviewer afterward. Actually, the anonymous donor was Woodruff, the head of the Coca Cola Company.)

The next year Allen tried again. He pared down the proposal drastically and promised that a way would be found to retire the bonds without increasing taxes. This time the vote against the bonds on the south side was not so heavy and the proposal passed easily.

Allen's strategy for holding the alliance together into the next election and beyond is a simple one. He means by a show of firmness and good will to keep the respect of both the business-led middle-class whites and the Negroes, and in this way to make himself the only candidate that either group can support. The policy calls for making himself the master rather than the servant of public opinion. In his campaign for election Allen employed a professional pollster to make three samplings of opinion, but he has not made any public opinion poll since. "I'm not trying to win a popularity contest," he says, "I do what I think is right." He has thought it right to employ Negroes as firemen (they had long been employed as policemen), to desegregate municipal swimming pools in response to a court order, to labor energetically behind the scenes to persuade hotel and restaurant owners to desegregate, to endorse the pending federal civil rights bill, and to appoint several Negroes to important jobs. His Negro appointees are all "doves," wealthy, middle-aged or older, and in a position to deliver votes. As for the young militants, the "hawks," he has warned them that the city will not tolerate violence or bow to ultimatums or threats.

So far the mayor's strategy seems to be working. There is a possibility, however, that in the next few years a good share of the "doves" in the Negro electorate may turn into "hawks." If that happens, the alliance will fail and business will not be so good in Atlanta. On the other hand, if the business community does enough to increase job opportunities for Negroes and to desegregate the community, many of the "hawks" may become "doves."

BOSTON:

The New Hurrah

In some ways Bostonians have not changed much since 1945 when they elected James Michael Curley, who had served two terms in jail, mayor for the fourth and last time. They are still poor (next to Pittsburgh, Boston has the lowest median family income of any large city outside the South); they are still renters rather than owners (a fact which may account for a phenomenally high per capita rate of municipal expenditure); and they are still overwhelmingly Irish. In at least one respect, however, they have changed fundamentally: today no man suspected of being a rascal has any chance of being elected mayor. Since Curley's time a new generation has come upon the scene, one which is embarrassed rather than amused by politicians of his sort. (The last time he ran, however, Curley got a heavier vote from voters in their twenties than from any other age group.) Boston has repeatedly shown a decided taste for conservatism, even austerity, in city government. How long it will continue to do so no one, of course, can say. For more than a decade it has been losing its middle class, which was small to begin with, to the suburbs. Eventually the people who remain in the central city may get fed up with good government and throw the rascals back in. So far, however, there is no sign of this happening.

Population and Economy

Compared to most central cities, Boston is a small part of its metropolitan area. The metropolitan area includes seventy-six cities and towns with a total population of 2,589,-301 (1960) and occupies 969 square miles. Boston proper occupies 47.8 square miles and has (1965) a population es-

timated at about 645,000. This is about 50,000 less than the
1960 census showed, and that figure in turn was 13 per cent
less than in 1950. The population of the metropolitan area
as a whole increased by 7 per cent between 1950 and 1960
and is still growing. Between 1950 and 1960, the city's population decreased by 13 per cent, while that of the metropolitan area increased by 7 per cent.

Boston has a higher percentage of persons of foreign
stock than any large city except New York. Most Bostonians
live in communities with a fairly well-defined ethnic character. Persons of Irish descent (a wider category than the
census' "foreign stock," since the Irish have been in Boston
in large numbers for more than two generations) comprise
more than half the population; the Irish live everywhere in
the city, but especially in South Boston, Charlestown, Ja-
maica Plain, Dorchester, and Brighton. South Boston is the
historic heart of Irish Boston; thousands who no longer
live there speak nostalgically of "the old neighborhood."
Italians are the second most numerous recent immigrant
group; about 8 per cent of the population is Italian ("foreign stock," not descent). Italians are concentrated in the
North End, where they comprise more than 90 per cent of
the population, and in East Boston. Jews (about 11 per cent
of the population in 1960) live mostly in Dorchester, Mat-
tapan, Allston, and Brighton. Practically all of the Negroes
(9 per cent of the population in 1960) live in Roxbury and
the adjoining South End. Yankees predominate in the Back
Bay-Beacon Hill area. Since 1960 the percentage of Jews
has decreased slightly and that of Negroes has increased
slightly.

About two-thirds of the church-affiliated population is
Roman Catholic.

Employment in Boston is concentrated in retail trade,
public services (government, schools, hospitals, transportation), and manufacturing (especially textiles and electrical
machinery). The employment base is so diversified that
there is no need to fear sudden mass unemployment. The
outlook for the central city is not particularly good, however. Boston is too close to New York to have much future
as a port or as an office headquarters for national firms.

Much commerce and manufacturing has moved to the suburbs, some of which, if boundary lines had not been drawn a century ago, would doubtless be part of the central city today.

How the Government Is Organized

Under a charter adopted in 1949, Boston has a strong mayor and a nine-man council, all elected at large. Previously it had had a twenty-two-member ward-based council.

THE MAYOR

The mayor serves a four-year term at a salary of $20,000. He appoints and removes department heads and board members, prepares the budget, initiates ordinances, and exercises a veto. In matters involving money he has an item veto which cannot be overridden; in other matters his veto may be overriden by a vote of six.

As of 1965, there are over 13,000 employees in the departments that are under the control of the mayor. Employees in departments *not* under the control of the mayor number somewhat less than 8,000. About half of these are teachers.

THE CITY COUNCIL

The council members are elected for two-year terms and are paid $7,500. The mayor may summon the council and address it when he pleases, and the council may require him or his department heads to furnish information in writing or to appear in person to answer questions. In practice, a mayor rarely asks to see the council, but it calls upon his administration for information fairly often. Both the mayor and the council may initiate ordinances, loans, land sales, and other measures "for the welfare of the city." The council can, of course, refuse to accept recommendations made by the mayor, but it cannot appropriate out of general revenues more than he recommends. The council elects its president each year. He presides, appoints committees, and serves as acting mayor. Much of the council's business is done in committee. It has little power over appointments, naming only the city clerk and a small council staff itself; the only mayoral appointments that it confirms are those of constables, weighers of goods, and members of the Housing and Redevelopment Authorities.

THE ELECTORATE

Spending and tax propositions come before the electorate only on the rare occasions when they are placed on the ballot by the state legislature.

INDEPENDENT AGENCIES

When Yankee Republicans found themselves hopelessly outnumbered in Boston by Irish Democrats they withdrew to the state legislature and exercised control over the city from there. For this reason, some functions normally performed by cities are performed in Boston by state agencies. A Finance Commission, appointed by the governor after consultation with the mayor, maintains continuous scrutiny of city affairs; it has the power of subpoena and may investigate anything. Liquor sales in Boston are regulated by a state licensing board, as are amusement and dining places.

Certain other functions are carried on by boards on which Boston, the suburbs, and the state are all represented. The Massachusetts Bay Transit Authority is one of these; the Metropolitan District Commission, which provides water, sewage disposal, and parks for Boston and some suburbs, is another.

A five-member School Committee is elected for two-year terms. Its members are unpaid. If the school budget is more than it was in the previous year, the mayor must approve the excess. Since it regularly exceeds the limit by a great deal, he has a considerable amount of indirect control over school affairs.

How It Really Works

A mayor of Boston is often harassed by the city council and sometimes he is checked by it in important matters. 'n

1963 and 1964, for example, the council slowed down the mayor's extensive urban renewal program and curtailed it in some residential areas. The mayor can only rarely use the carrot-and-stick approach; usually he has no stick and some councilmen have not much appetite for such carrots as he can offer. Because they are elected at large there is not much he can do either to help them or to hurt them. (In Boston it is not the practice to give councilmen credit or blame for local public works.) If the more experienced and aggressive councilmen disagree with the mayor or bear him a grudge, they can make his life miserable.

Perhaps the mayor's greatest advantage in dealing with the council is its own incapacity. Few councilmen have the time, interest, or ability to suggest policy innovations or to criticize in a serious way the policies of the administration. Here, for example, is an account given by Councillor Thomas A. Sullivan of his experience as chairman of a sub-committee to review a city budget of more than $100 million: *

When a department head came in, the usual question was: "How are you, Joe? Is there enough money for personnel in your budget? . . ."

The first witness at my first hearing was the police commissioner.

"Commissioner," I said, "would you like to give us the broad outlines of your program for the year ahead?"

"No," he said, "I would not."

That was the tone of most of the hearings. . . .

Usually one or two other councillors sat with me. Their contribution was largely social—calling people by their first names. When I would manage to work a witness into some kind of a pocket with questions about where the money was going, some councilman would interrupt.

"May I ask a question, Mr. Chairman?"

"Certainly."

"Joe, how do you manage to do such a fine job on so little money."

* Sullivan was speaking to a class at Harvard College.

"It isn't easy, but we try. . . ."

When the hearings were over, I recommended about $500,000 in cuts. It was amusing to see what happened. The committee members were whimsical; they'd give me a cut for no reason at all, except, you know—"he's not a bad guy after all"—and then they'd deny me the next one. In that way they cut the $500,000 down to about $200,000 in committee. Then on the floor that was cut down to about $100,000.

Occasionally the council spots an unpopular item in the mayor's budget and gives it the axe. In both 1963 and 1964, for example, it drastically reduced the amount asked for purchase of police cars (Bostonians are ardently in favor of "putting the cop back on the beat") and in 1964 cut an aerial survey requested by the urban renewal agency. For the most part, however, there is no political mileage to be made by cutting the budget.

The state legislature is also difficult for a mayor to deal with. Boston has slightly more representation in the legislature than its population warrants, but its mayors find the going there hard just the same. Mayor John B. Hynes (1949-1959) apparently gave up in despair: he seldom asked the legislature for anything. Mayor John F. Collins prepares a legislative program with great care, keeps two lobbyists working for it in the State House, has selected legislators in for coffee and doughnuts, and at the end of the session has got some—but not very much—of what he asked. Even when the governor is a Democrat, the mayor of Boston does not get much from the state. One reason for this is that the mayor, as mayor, is a nonpartisan politician. Another is that some of the party men from Boston in the legislature are his rivals, or at any rate want the city run their way rather than his. (During Collins' first term the president of the state senate was the man he had defeated in the mayoralty election.)

How They Get Elected

Elections have been nonpartisan since the adoption of a reform charter in 1909. They are held in odd-numbered years. A council and a school committee are chosen at every election, and a mayor at every other one. A preliminary election is held late in September. To get on the ballot, mayoralty candidates must file petitions with 3,000 signatures and council candidates petitions with 1,500 signatures. All but two mayoralty candidates and all but eighteen council candidates are eliminated in the preliminary. The final, or run-off, election is held six weeks later, early in November.

In the first election after the adoption of the reform charter (1910) John F. ("Honey Fitz") Fitzgerald, President Kennedy's grandfather, defeated a Yankee in a close and bitter race and established the rule of the Irish. The only non-Irish candidate to have made a serious bid since was an Italian who ran against Collins in 1963. He carried only three wards and got 40 per cent of the vote.

Although both national parties are organized on a ward and precinct basis, neither endorses or finances candidates for city office. However, individuals prominent in the parties—especially the Republican party—frequently do participate in the local campaigns. For example, the chairman of the Republican city committee used the committee's letterhead in urging support for John E. Powers, Collins' opponent in his first race for mayor.

As it operates in Boston, nonpartisanship gives Republicans (but not the Republican party) and independents more weight than they would otherwise have. Registered Democrats outnumber registered Republicans by more than 6 to 1. The nonpartisan primary is therefore like an open Democratic primary except in one very important respect: some 100,000 Republicans and independents who could not vote in a Democratic primary *can* vote in a nonpartisan one. Thus, although all of the candidates may be Democrats (only once since 1909 has a Republican been elected mayor), they will be Democrats who must compete for the votes of the Republicans and the independents.

As one would expect, candidates for mayor cast their nets

as wide as possible. Campaign platforms are broad enough
for everyone to stand on, and candidates make much of
their bipartisanship as well as their nonpartisanship.

In some nonpartisan cities politicians who run for local
(nonpartisan) office belong to a different set than those
who run for county, state, and national (partisan) office. In
Boston, however, there is a good deal of movement between
city and state offices. Curley was elected governor, all five
candidates for mayor in the 1959 preliminary election had
served in the legislature, and Mayor Collins is expected to
try for a seat in the United States Senate some day.

Lacking both patronage and party support, candidates for
mayor must catch the eye of the public as best they can.
Each sponsors several large rallies and all buy a good deal of
television and radio time and newspaper space, plaster the
city with billboards, bumper stickers, posters, and brochures,
and fill its air with sound-truck oratory. Since this must be
done twice—once for a preliminary and then again for a
general election—campaigns are expensive. In 1959 Powers
reported expenses of $203,540 and Collins of $164,546.
These figures mean little, however, for Massachusetts law
does not require a complete accounting and not much attention is paid to the law anyway. Insiders say that Powers'
campaign cost at least $500,000. Much of the money comes
from testimonial banquets. (Powers is said to have raised
$240,000 in a single evening.) The big contributors are in-
surance brokers, contractors, and others who hope to do business with the city, and large property owners who think
that they may be protecting themselves against increases in
their assessments.

It goes without saying that most councillors are Irish. Of
the fifty-seven men who have been elected between 1951
(when the at-large system went into effect) and 1963, nine
have been Italian and the rest Irish. The winning Italians
have been men whose reputations for honesty enabled them
to pick up many Yankee and Jewish votes; those whose appeal was narrowly ethnic ("North End types") have lost.
Negroes are not numerous enough to win a place on the
council. In 1959 a Negro finished fifteenth in a field of

eighteen. No Negro has run since. Jews and Yankees have even less chance of being elected and seldom try.

In council races, incumbents rarely lose. Campaigns are therefore seldom very vigorous, elaborate, or expensive. Issues are not important, and the newspapers pay little attention to council campaigns. The candidates and their friends pass out cards and brochures, travel around in sound trucks, and make brief appearances at meetings and rallies. Usually the best a challenger can hope for is to be the lucky one who picks off the weakest incumbent or to head the list of also-rans, thus putting himself in line for succession if a vacancy occurs between elections. The challenger's big problem is to differentiate himself from the rest of the field, which may number as many as forty, and to make his name known beyond the confines of his own ward. Having a name that is resoundingly Irish does not suffice to attract attention, since there are always many candidates with such names. Having a particularly well-known Irish name may make the difference, however: in 1963 the son of former mayor Hynes won a place on the council on the strength of his name. Being the only woman on the ballot may also help: this may account for the success of another challenger in 1963.

When an incumbent does lose, it is likely to be because many things went wrong simultaneously. The case of Thomas A. Sullivan, the councillor quoted above, is illustrative. He was regarded by the press and the "good government" forces as by far the best man on the council; nevertheless he lost by seventy-three votes in 1963. His main troubles seem to have been first, that as an incumbent with strong press support he was overconfident and did not campaign hard. A second Sullivan was on the ballot, and the confusion of names worked to Thomas Sullivan's disadvantage; he was also unlucky enough to draw a place near the bottom of the ballot. Furthermore, although Sullivan was on the full slate of candidates endorsed by the "good government" people, the endorsement of so many others tended to take votes from him. The teachers' vote (Sullivan was a former teacher and the teachers had been solidly behind him) was split over the issue of collective bargaining. Finally, in 1963 there were more serious challengers than usual.

Civic associations, labor unions, and newspapers do not play a large part in the election of councilmen. In the main, a candidate makes his appeal not as the representative of some organized interest (such as the labor unions or home-owners' associations) but as a "personality." When in office, therefore, he is not very susceptible to the discipline, or in-fluence, of such organizations; on the contrary, his role as a "personality" permits and even encourages him to take an eccentric approach to the policy problems that come before him. By tradition the council is not a stepping stone to higher elective or appointive office. This not only discour-ages able men from running for the council but also encour-ages irresponsibility on the part of successful candidates. For one reason or another, at any rate, the council usually has more than its fair share of hacks and less than its fair share of statesmen.

In mayoralty elections voter turn-out is between 60 and 70 per cent of those registered. When there is no mayoralty contest, it is about half that. In the thirties, when council-men were elected on a ward basis, turn-out in nonmayoralty years averaged about 55 per cent. After the substitution of the at-large system for the ward-based one, it declined stead-ily, settling at 33 per cent in 1957 and again in 1961. Ap-parently many voters think there is less at stake in council elections now than there used to be, and in this they are surely right.

Interest Groups and Influentials

BUSINESS

Before 1910, when "Honey Fitz" was elected mayor, Yankee businessmen ran the city government as a matter of course. Since then they have been on the outside looking in, most often from the suburbs. They never run for local office and they seldom participate in local elections, except for buying "protection" with campaign contributions. Long-standing distrust between the Yankee-Protestant-Republican and the

Irish-Catholic-Democrat—and therefore between business-men and "pols" (politicians)—has prevented much collaboration. In recent years, however, the ice has begun to melt. Nowadays not very many of the leading businessmen are "Brahmins" or even natives of Boston. Among the politicians, also, there have been changes. Mayor Collins is perfectly self-confident in his dealings with the businessmen. Now and then he makes a sly, tongue-in-cheek reference to the alleged statesmanlike qualities of Yankee businessmen; but he and they are on terms of mutual respect.

THE PRESS

Boston is one of the very few cities having competitive daily newspapers. There are two morning and evening combines: the *Globe* papers (morning circ. 202,711; evening 144,855; Sunday 488,105) and the *Herald and Traveller* (morning circ. 176,483; evening 161,453; Sunday 281,586). There are also the morning Hearst *Record American* (441,810) and the church-owned *Christian Science Monitor* (the circulation of which is national). Only New York, with ten times Boston's population, has as many newspapers. All of the commercial newspapers tend to favor "soft" local news (crime, disaster, fires, traffic accidents, and "human interest"); thus treatment of serious local news is generally superficial. In other cities nonpartisan politics enhances the influence of the press; not so in Boston. The city's papers do not crusade or take much part in city campaigns; their influence on voters is apparently slight. No Boston paper has ever won a Pulitzer prize for reporting, and none has won one for public service since 1923.

There seem to be several reasons why the commercial press does not do a better job and wield more influence. One is bitter competition for circulation and advertising: the papers have to give readers what they want, not what they "ought to have." Another is Boston's nearness to New York: many people who would normally demand serious local news read the *New York Times,* which reaches Boston in plenty of time for breakfast. Finally, the monopolization of local politics by the "pols" and the lower middle class tends to reduce the interest and participation of newspapers, just as it does that of other business interests and of the upper middle class in general.

LABOR

Organized labor in Boston has a large membership, money, and politically skilled leaders. One might therefore expect it to play an important part in city politics. Actually it does not. In part this is because so many matters are decided by the state rather than the city that the unions concentrate their attention on the legislature; in part it is because the labor movement is pragmatic and conservative rather than ideological and radical. The building trades unions dominate it through the Central Labor Council of the AFL-CIO. A Committee on Political Education (COPE), an arm of the State Labor Council, AFL-CIO, endorses candidates for office and can put 300 to 400 workers in the field at election time. The COPE workers do not live in the precincts, however; they are sent into them when occasion arises and are probably less effective than they might be for this reason. In addition, the monopolization of politics by the "pols" probably reduces the influence of the unions, as it does that of other organizations. "Labor doesn't pick the candidates," a labor man said. "They pick themselves, and individual unions support their favorite nominees." Mayor Collins' opponent in his first race, the then Senate President John E. Powers, had wholehearted backing from all the unions, but was badly beaten just the same.

THE NEGRO

The position of the Negro in Boston is paradoxical. The city was the cradle of the abolition movement, and it has had a Negro community for well over a century. (When the Irish arrived, the well-established Negroes regarded them as inferiors.) Massachusetts has enacted more legislation on behalf of the Negro than any other state and it is the only state that has elected a Negro to high office (the attorney-generalship). Nevertheless, Negroes are more passive politically in Boston than in any other major city.

Many Negroes do not vote, and of those who do many do not vote for "race" candidates. The Negro who ran for the council in 1959 got his heaviest vote from people—white as well as black—who regarded him as a neighborhood favorite son. Outside of his own ward, the percentage of Negroes voting for him was not much higher than that of the whites. He estimated later that at least 3,000 Negroes who voted did not vote for him.

The national stir over civil rights has had some effect in Boston. The Boston chapter of the NAACP took a "tough" position on *de facto* segregation in 1963 and vowed to defeat at the polls a school committee chairman who refused to discuss the issue. (She was reelected by a landslide.) CORE and the NAACP held a two-day sit-in in the school committee offices, and an *ad hoc* organization of college students led a fairly successful "selective patronage" campaign against a baking company. By the standards of other big cities, however, the Boston Negro community is still passive. Some think this is because it is still too small to provide enough highly motivated young people to constitute a "critical mass." Others think it is because Yankees and Jews have done the talking for the Negroes for so long that they have never grown accustomed to talking for themselves. Still others think it is because the "upper crust" of the Negro community is separated from the rest of it by a distance even greater than in other cities.

How Issues Are Handled

Boston was in serious financial trouble in 1959 when Mayor Collins was first elected. It was forced by the legislature to depend almost exclusively upon the property tax, the yield of which had been falling, while expenditures had risen fast. Between 1949 and 1959 the city's tax rate had doubled. Collins was tough from the start. He denied the School Committee funds it said it needed, and reduced the number of full-time city employees. After four years the tax rate, which had been $101.20 when he took office, was down to $96. The mayor meanwhile had started a huge urban renewal program. He began by hiring an administrator who had made a reputation with renewal in New Haven; this man soon shook $76,860,000 in grants out of the federal government and had dramatic projects under way all over the city.

Economy and urban renewal, one might think, would have been the central issues when Collins came up for re-election. It was at least arguable that the mayor should have improved schools no matter what happened to the tax rate; it was also at least arguable that he should have made even more drastic cuts. Renewal (one might think) was bound to be discussed from every side. It touched the lives of thousands of people directly, it was changing the character of the city for all time, and it had never been tested at the polls.

As it turned out, neither economy nor renewal was discussed seriously during the campaign. The mayor's opponents on the council (some were candidates to succeed him) claimed that he had not really cut taxes, and they formed a majority which twice rejected the final plans for the Government Center, the most important single project in the whole renewal program. What they talked about mainly was that the Mayor had levied a small sewer tax, placed a charge of one cent on soap and towels in the L Street Bathhouse, gone out of the city to hire the urban renewal administrator, and failed to improve garbage collection. ("You can close the libraries and burn down the schools, but have those garbage trucks there three times a morning and you are guaranteed reelection—unless you ask people to roll out their own barrels," a sardonic council candidate said just before the election.)

That Boston's big issues are not seriously debated at election time does not, of course, mean that the voters do not take them into account. Collins was reelected, after all, by a plurality larger than before. His opponent, to be sure, was not a very strong candidate. But this in itself may have reflected general satisfaction with the mayor's handling of major matters, for if he had not handled these matters well, a stronger candidate would doubtless have appeared and would have gotten more newspaper support and more campaign contributions from businessmen than the man who did run. Nevertheless, no matter how well he does with big matters, a Boston mayor neglects small ones—garbage collection, for example—at his peril.

DETROIT:

Balancing Act

Conflict runs deep in Detroit. The United Automobile Workers, one of the most militant unions in the country, confronts the Big Three motor companies a hundred times a day. A large and growing Negro population with more than its share of extremists (it was in Detroit that the Black Muslim movement got started) presses angrily against lower-middle-class Polish and Irish neighborhoods that are determined not to give it entry. Owners of small homes with big mortgages seethe with resentment against the welfare state and its special beneficiaries. Fear of unemployment is always present (if people stop buying cars, Detroit shuts down), and this fear contributes to the tension.

In the 1940's all these factors made for a politics of hate.[1] The left and right fought bitterly in election after election. Finally the left gave up trying to take control, and the city has been governed ever since by conservative businessmen and moderate politicians. Somehow they have managed to maintain a balance among the bitterly antagonistic interests; for a city of its size and character, Detroit has for many years been remarkably tranquil and well governed.

Population and Economy

The city has been trying, with some success, to diversify its economic base in order to reduce the threat of unemployment. Essentially, however, it is still a one-industry town (the auto companies employ 14 per cent of the metropolitan area's labor force) and is likely to be so for some time to come. The demand for cars and the policies of the

[1] (See C. O. Smith and S. B. Sarasohn, "Hate Propaganda in Detroit," *Public Opinion Quarterly*, Vol. X, 1946-47, pp. 24-52.)

companies and the unions are therefore matters of urgent public interest. Auto workers are highly paid (Detroit's median family income is high—$6,069 in 1959—and so is its rate of home ownership), but they are also extremely vulnerable to swings in the business cycle; during the recession of 1960, one worker in ten was without a job. The knowledge that that could happen again is a constant source of anxiety to the mortgage-payers.

High-paying industrial work has brought Negroes, Southern whites, and foreigners to the city in large numbers. The increase in population from these sources has been more than offset, however, by the movement of the middle class to the suburbs. The population in 1960 was 1,670,144, 10 per cent less than in 1950. In this period the number of Negroes increased by 30 per cent, from 303,721 to 478,-174. The Negro "invasion" of the "nice neighborhoods" being vacated by the middle-class whites is still going on and is one of the most conspicuous facts of life in the city.

Of the whites who lived in the city in 1960, 32 per cent were of foreign stock, mainly Poles, Czechs, Germans, Italians, and Canadians. The Poles and the Czechs have a particularly high rate of home ownership and a marked distaste for public expenditures of all kinds, especially those that would increase property taxes. They also seem to have a particularly strong antipathy to the Negro.

How the Government Is Organized

Detroit has the strong-mayor-council form of government. It elects a mayor, city clerk, city treasurer, and councilmen every four years. The mayor, whose salary is $25,000, is probably the strongest in the country. In addition to the usual powers of a strong mayor, he appoints and removes department heads *without cause,* has an item veto (which can, however, be overridden) over all acts of the council, and is in sole charge of licensing. "There are no generals in my departments," a recent mayor remarked with satisfaction, "only sergeants."

The council is also strong. It consists of nine members all elected at large at the same time for four-year terms. Members are paid for full-time service ($12,000 a year plus an additional $750 for serving as county supervisors); they meet every weekday as a committee of the whole. The council may enact ordinances, levy taxes, appropriate money, authorize bond issues, make investigations, and prefer charges against elected or appointed officials other than judges. To override the mayor's veto in a financial matter, seven votes are required; in other matters, only six are required.

SCHOOLS

Schools are run by a seven-member Board of Education elected at large for six-year terms.

THE COUNTY

Wayne County, which includes nineteen cities, sixteen townships, and eight incorporated villages, is governed by a 111-member Board of Supervisors on which sit fifty-eight of the principal elected and appointed officials of Detroit. The nearest thing to a county executive is a three-member Board of Auditors elected on a partisan basis for four-year terms. The powers of the county are very limited, and it has trouble raising revenue for routine needs. For these reasons it does not obstruct the city government.

THE ELECTORATE

Charter amendments and propositions may be submitted to the electorate by the council or by petition. In practice, few matters are decided by referendum.

How It Really Works

In fact as well as in law the mayor is the mainspring of Detroit city government. He has very little patronage to bestow: about thirty-five salaried jobs and 250 unpaid but more or less prestigious commissionerships. He gets most of his informal influence from his ability to form and give expression to public opinion. His views and doings are always news, and this enables him to dominate the discussion of any issue. Detroit mayors have so much power and receive so much attention that they tend, some say, to develop Napoleonic complexes.

Councilmen have no patronage at all—even their secretaries are under civil service. They have more weight than the councilmen of most cities, however, because, being full-time, they know enough about the city's business to be taken seriously. A department head called before the council to discuss a budgetary question, for example, cannot rely upon the ignorance or inattention of the councilmen to save him from having to get down to brass tacks. Being elected at large rather than from wards, the councilmen have little incentive to ask the departments or the mayor to favor particular neighborhoods or small groups of voters. There are occasions, nevertheless, when the administration can help a councilman with his constituents and the councilmen, of course, take this into account in their relations with department heads and, to a lesser extent, with the mayor himself.

The council is by no means a rubber stamp. It sometimes initiates action on important matters, and now and then it demonstrates its independence by defying the mayor. Generally speaking, however, the mayor has his way in matters he considers really important. His budget, for example, is changed only in minor respects.

The mayor's ascendancy over the council can be explained in part, by the absence of stable voting blocs within it. This, in turn, is a function of the nonpartisan, at-large system by which councilmen are elected. In the absence of parties, candidates for the council must find ways of making their names known to the public. For incumbents, one tried and true way is to attack the mayor; another is to be the center of a row within the council. It is no accident, then, that the councilmen tend to be mavericks and "loners." Needless to say, this way of doing things reduces the collective influence of the council. When every councilman strains to make his voice heard above all the others, the effect is to drown out all the council voices, leaving the mayor's the only one that can be heard. The councilmen are well aware of this, but the nature of the system does not allow them to behave differently.

How They Get Elected

The mayor and council are elected in the year following a presidential election. A nonpartisan primary is held in September and a general election in November. The two candidates for mayor who poll the most votes in the primary run against each other in the general election, as do the eighteen leading candidates for council. The council candidate who gets the most votes in the general election becomes council president.

Elections are nonpartisan not only in the sense that party affiliations do not appear on the ballot, but also in the sense that the national parties do not finance or otherwise assist any of the candidates. The nearest thing to a political party in local elections is the AFL-CIO Committee on Political Education (COPE), which drafts a platform, endorses candidates, and sends rank-and-file union members out to do precinct work at election time. It has not had much success, however, in delivering votes in local (as distinguished from state and national) elections.

There being no party labels to go by, most voters have a hard time deciding which candidate stands for what. This is especially true in primaries, where the number of candidates is sometimes very large. (Once there were 191; in 1961, a more normal year, there were 50.) Frequently voters solve their problem by choosing candidates whose names sound familiar. These tend to be incumbents. In the forty-five years after the adoption of the present charter in 1918, only twenty-two councilmen running for reelection were defeated. Occasionally a challenger has a name that people recognize, or think they recognize, and this may turn the trick for him. A councilman named James Brickley, for example, is supposed to have benefited from confusion with the television news commentator David Brinkley. Several Murphys sit on city and county courts, thanks, apparently, to the popularity of the late Frank Murphy, a mayor who became governor and then a justice of the United States Supreme Court.

Some observers think that nonpartisanship gives conservative candidates a decided advantage. One theory on the subject holds that in the absence of parties public-spirited motives must be relied upon as a basis for campaign organization; such motives, the theory asserts, exist mainly among relatively well-educated, upper-income people who tend to be conservative. Although this theory has a certain plausibility, it fails to take account of COPE, the existence of which is ample proof that conservatives are not the only ones who can organize. According to another theory, the conservatives benefit from the separation that the nonpartisan system makes between local issues on the one hand and state and national ones on the other. If the Democratic party took part in local elections, says this theory, it would exert some discipline over voters who now vote for conservatives. Or (to frame the argument somewhat differently) if voters had to choose between an ideological Republican position and an ideological Democratic one, the latter would win hands down. But this assumes that the local Democratic party would not be split or would not fall into the hands of conservatives, an assumption which may not be realistic.

In order to be elected to the council, a candidate must get a certain number of votes from a wide sector of the electorate. He must also, however, get very active support, including financial backing, from one or two, or even two or three, city-wide interests. The list on page 57 characterizes the councilmen who were serving in 1964 and shows each one's base of support.

One can easily see from this list that most of the major interests in the city are represented on the council.

A candidate for mayor, since he faces one opponent instead of a whole field in the general election, must have a very broad base of support. It is not enough to have labor behind him, or Negroes, or homeowners; he must have strong support from every, or almost every, important group within the electorate. He depends to a certain extent upon newspapers and civic organizations to rally these voters behind him. While there can be little doubt that normally the newspapers and the civic organizations can help him with their readers, members, and followers, they cannot

Councillor	*Base of Support*
Former baseball player	Homeowner's associations
Woman lawyer	Persons of Eastern European stock, especially members of the Greek Orthodox Church; business and professional women; bowling leagues
Former city accountant	Persons of Polish stock; the economy-minded; "good government" forces, including the newspapers
Former policeman, once head of the Community Relations Bureau	Organized policemen; also, to begin with, Negroes and liberals; later, homeowners' associations
Former labor leader (UAW)	COPE
Professor of sociology at Wayne State University	Union-Negro-liberal coalition
Young businessman, a former F.B.I. agent	Young Irish-Catholic businessmen and professionals
Lawyer active in county politics	Building trades unions; Negroes
Negro lawyer	NAACP, various unions, and liberal white organizations

"deliver" votes in the manner of a political machine, and the candidate who takes too seriously the endorsement of the various "leaders" of opinion may find himself defeated by someone who addresses himself to the voters directly.

This was dramatically the case in the election of 1961. Mayor Louis C. Miriani had the support of all the important organizations. Both metropolitan newspapers backed him, as did COPE and the Building Trades Council, the Citizens' League (a "good government" organization), the most prominent Negro leaders, and the principal businessmen (Henry Ford 2d took the unusual step of issuing a statement endorsing him). Miriani lost heavily, however, to thirty-three-year-old Jerome P. Cavanagh, whose only supporters were the firefighters, a few of the less prestigious labor and Negro leaders, and numerous young people at the University of Detroit, the Jesuit institution from which he had graduated not very long before. Cavanagh won by going over the heads of the "leaders" and making his appeal to the ordinary voter. Television made this possible. The viewers saw a vigorous, forceful, charming man, and they were captivated by his directness and freshness. His opponent, he told them, was a tool of the "big interests" (the newspapers, the motor companies, and the labor unions); the time had come for the "little guy" to assert himself by taking the city government out of the hands of the selfish little group of professionals that had been running it so long.

Cavanagh's campaign cost practically nothing by Detroit standards—about $50,000 for both the primary and the runoff, he estimated later. Some of the money came from businessmen who were so irked by the Miriani administration that they were willing to contribute to a sure loser in the hope of embarrassing it. Cavanagh himself was perfectly certain that he would win, however, and he and a few close friends put up their own money and even borrowed on personal notes to buy television time.

Although Cavanagh's vigor, charm, and astuteness were indispensable to his success, he also had some help from his opponent. About a year before the election, the police, in searching for two murderers, infuriated the Negro community by indiscriminately picking up some 1,500 Negroes who were then released without charges. For this Mayor Miriani, rightly or wrongly, was blamed. Then, a month or so before the general election, the council defeated by a 5 to 4 vote a proposal by the Negro councilman to strengthen the Commission on Human Relations. The mayor failed to take a stand in support of this proposal, and Negro opinion was further outraged. If the mayor thought that what offended the Negroes would gratify white homeowners (a much more numerous group, of course), he was wrong. Detroit at that time was suffering severely from unemployment, and the homeowners seemed to think that the mayor was partly to blame for it. When he failed to find a way to reduce the property tax, they too deserted him. The city employees were also dissatisfied; the mayor had flatly refused to raise their pay.

Interest Groups and Influentials

BUSINESS

Although they are greatly interested in state and federal tax and labor laws, the national corporations with offices and plants in Detroit (especially General Motors, Ford, and Chrysler) take little part in local politics. It is the firms that are tied to the city—department stores, banks, utilities, office buildings, and newspapers—that are most concerned with local affairs, and together, they exercise a great deal of influence—aided by the nonpartisan system, for without parties to raise campaign funds, every candidate needs business friends.

More than in most large cities, perhaps, businessmen in Detroit are in the habit of supporting political ventures from motives that are not narrowly business-serving. One reason may be that in Detroit there is not the usual social chasm between the principal businessmen and the principal officeholders; the city's principal officials are not snubbed by the businessmen. Another reason may be that the businessmen feel united by pressure from a common foe—the unions.

THE CITIZENS' LEAGUE

Business and professional men run the Citizens' League, an organization of 3,000 persons which screens candidates and publishes endorsements in its bulletin, the *Civic Searchlight,* and in the daily press. Some politicians say that a "preferred" rating is worth 10,000 to 70,000 votes, most of them in two well-to-do wards. The *Civic Searchlight* is distributed by businesses to their employees (the Big Three motor companies give it only to salaried employees) and by many Protestant churches. The League has always had a close connection with the Detroit Council of Churches. Its membership was once almost entirely Protestant; now, however, it includes many Catholics and Jews.

CITY EMPLOYEES

There are more than 20,000 city employees; along with their relatives and friends, they constitute a powerful voting bloc. The directness of their interest in wages and hours, conditions of work, and other aspects of city policy makes their influence particularly great.

THE PRESS

Detroit's two daily newspapers play an influential and generally conservative role. The morning *Free Press* (daily circ. 509,000; Sundays 561,000) is one of the Knight chain. The publisher of the evening *News* (daily circ. 702,000; Sundays 914,000) is Peter B. Clark, a Ph.D. in political science from the University of Chicago (he wrote his dissertation in 1959 on "The Chicago Big Businessman as a Civic Leader"). Both papers have always energetically opposed union candidates for mayor. Their endorsements are thought to have a good deal of effect on middle-class voters; other voters, however, tend to regard them as part of a malevolent, big business conspiracy. Mayor Cavanagh was more than half serious when he told an interviewer that he takes pains to get plenty of criticism, as well as praise, from the press.

The *Free Press* and the *News* are firmly committed to the nonpartisan system, which, of course, gives them more influence than they would otherwise have. Neither newspaper is much given to crusading, but both have a commitment to "good government" which leads them to support certain public improvements. Whether because they think the principles of "good government" require it or to forestall something worse ("radical trouble-makers"), they have supported some council candidates—a UAW official and an ultraliberal college professor, for example—with whose general views they must be altogether out of sympathy. The newspapers helped elect a Negro to the council in 1961.

LABOR

Despite their big membership, tight organization, and militant spirit, COPE and the left-wing unions have had little success in city politics. Several councilmen are "friends of labor," but the UAW and its allies have never elected a mayor or even backed a winning candidate. In the 1940's they made three all-out efforts to elect their own left-wing candidate, and each time they lost. In 1949, when a conservative businessman got 60 per cent of the vote, they decided to concentrate on state and national politics. Their efforts on the local scene have been half-hearted and ineffective ever since. They backed Miriani against Cavanagh, a more liberal candidate, because they thought Miriani would win and because the union leaders were on good personal terms with him. The nonpartisan system is probably one reason why COPE has not had more influence: many voters seem to think that for unions to put up candidates and carry on precinct work violates the spirit, if not the letter, of nonpartisanship.

The conservative Building Trades Council has had somewhat more success in local politics than COPE. Its objectives are very limited: to increase the amount of work for members (it joins enthusiastically with the left-wing unions in support of housing, school construction, sewer improvements, and other public works that will provide jobs for building trades workers), to control the appointment of housing and construction inspectors, and to have an inside track with the authorities when jurisdictional disputes arise. Any politician it can depend upon in these important matters is likely to have its support.

NEGROES

Of the several score Negro organizations in Detroit, the most important (listed, politically speaking, from right to left) are the following:

1.) The Urban League, led for forty-two years by a polished, soft-spoken graduate of Phillips Exeter Academy. He retired in 1960 and was succeeded by his assistant of many years, who is pushing for "positive discrimination" in employment.

2.) The Detroit branch of NAACP, which with 24,000 members is the largest in the country. It has had full-time, professional leadership since 1942, and has long been considered the protest arm of the Negro community. In the last several years, however, it has been criticized by other more militant groups.

3.) The Cotillion Club, which was organized for social purposes by a small group of professional and business people and has proved to be a training ground for leaders. The club inspires its members to use their money and position for public-serving endeavors. It launched a successful campaign for the election of a Negro councilman with a contribution of $4,000, and it helped elect the first Negro to the Board of Education. It was the first Negro organization to endorse Cavanagh's candidacy for mayor.

4.) The Trade Union Leadership Council (TULC), organized in 1957 by Horace L. Sheffield, a staff man in the UAW's citizenship department, to improve the economic position within their unions of the approximately 75,000 Detroit Negroes who are union members. TULC, the membership of which soon grew to more than 9,000, has raised money for the NAACP and has supported voter registration drives, neighborhood self-improvement projects, and other nonunion activities. Its main concern, however, is still with the internal affairs of the unions. Its newspaper, the *Vanguard,* is a mouthpiece for Sheffield, who is still one of its leading spirits. He and TULC were early and vigorous supporters of Cavanagh, and Sheffield is now one of the most influential Negroes in the city. A moderate, he changed the date of a street march in the summer of 1963 from a weekday to a Sunday and brought Dr. Martin Luther King to the city to overshadow certain inflammatory local speakers, thus helping to contain an explosive situation.

5.) The Group on Advanced Leadership (GOAL), which is both militant and nationalist. One of the principal leaders of GOAL is the Reverend Albert B. Cleague, Jr., pastor of the Central Congregational Church, who, with his two brothers and his sister, owns a printing plant and publishes the *Illustrated News,* a weekly which claims a circulation of 35,000. Through the columns of the *Illustrated News* Cleague has attacked not only the governor, the mayor, and the board of education, but also the Negro city councilman and the whole Negro establishment. According to him, the Negro leaders of Detroit "constitute a small group of friends who use the *Michigan Chronicle* [the largest Negro paper in the state, which carries a regular column by Sheffield] to perpetuate themselves and their friends as leaders."

There are several other militant organizations with small memberships consisting of students and a few white and Negro adults. These include the Congress on Racial Equality (CORE) and the Freedom Now Party, which ran a statewide slate in the November, 1964, election.

The militants are expected to put up a candidate for city council in the fall of 1965. He cannot win (to win a Negro must get many white votes, and he cannot get them without newspaper, union, and liberal endorsement), but he may, intentionally or otherwise, prevent a moderate Negro from being elected.

How Issues Are Handled

Although deeply torn by ideological and racial conflict and constantly in fear of mass unemployment, Detroit is an exceptionally well-governed city. Except for a lapse in 1938-40, when a mayor ended his term by going to jail, the city government has been honest and businesslike. And except for some awful days in 1943, when 31 persons were killed and more than 600 injured in a race riot, the mutual hatred of whites and Negroes has been held within bounds. By the standards that are reasonable to apply, race relations in Detroit are remarkably good.

Detroiters, voters as well as civic leaders, are aware that they live in a city packed with dynamite, and they do not play with matches. The left-wing unions, for example, do not try to take control of the city government. Similarly, the newspapers see to it that Negroes are represented on the council. Both the left and the right seem to be reconciled to government by moderates. This means less expenditure for community services and facilities than the liberals would like, but it also means lower taxes, and this, the liberals apparently recognize, is a price that must be paid to avoid a further accumulation of bitterness on the part of the home-owning, mortgage-paying lower middle class.

The stability of the system does not depend entirely upon self-conscious restraint, however. There are some built-in mechanisms—the office of mayor is the most important—which also tend to keep things steady. No matter what his personal views may be, an intelligent politician who wants to be mayor must act as a moderating force. To be elected in the first place, he must appeal to a wide variety of more or less opposed interests. If he is too closely identified with any one (say the unions), this factor in itself will make him unacceptable to others (say business) whose support he must have. An extremist of any sort, therefore, is ruled out from the start. Once in office, a mayor must create and maintain a coalition of all of the principal interests—Negroes, homeowning whites, labor, business, and the rest. He does this by giving each interest something that is important to it without being unduly offensive to the other, antagonistic interests. Here, for example, are some of the things Cavanagh did during his first three years in office:

Ordered the police to stop putting indiscriminate pressure on Negroes.

Appointed several Negroes to top positions.

Declared in favor of an open-occupancy ordinance.

Cut the budget for aid to dependent children. (He did this because he had to, but he got credit from anti-Negro whites just the same.)

Flatly refused to allow racial demonstrators to camp in city hall.

Reduced property taxes.

Imposed an income tax on residents and on suburbanites working in the city.

Raised the pay of key city employees.

Got $50 million for the city from the federal government.

Made numerous "blue ribbon" appointments to departments
and commissions.

Expanded the neighborhood conservation program.

While using these measures to create the coalition he
needed, Cavanagh cemented it by making the most of his
personal attributes—youth, Irish-Catholic background, ob-
vious intelligence, honesty, and seriousness of purpose. Five
nights a week he appeared before audiences: Negroes,
homeowners, liberals, unionists, Poles, city employees. There
was no group that he did not go out of his way to charm.
That a less-than-skillful player at this balancing game can
fail suddenly and completely is shown by the example of
Miriani. Possibly a highly skillful player can succeed in-
definitely. There is no reason to be confident of that, however; a time may come when no possible combination of
measures and no amount of charm will suffice to hold the
coalition together. And if it breaks apart, the dynamite may
go off.

EL PASO:

Two Cultures

El Paso children begin arithmetic by learning that "two plus *dos* equals fo'." The "two" is standard American, the *"dos"* is Mexican, and the "fo'" is Deep Southern. This mixture of cultures gives the city's politics, no less than its first-grade arithmetic, a special flavor. Mutual distrust between "Latins" (people of Mexican origin or descent) and "Anglos" (all others except Negroes) is a fundamental fact of life in El Paso. Among other things, it largely determines which candidates are elected and which policies are pursued. Sometimes it leads to unexpected results.

Population and Economy

El Paso is a boom town if there ever was one. Between 1950 and 1960 its population increased 112 per cent, to 276,687. The Army Air Defense Center at Fort Bliss and the White Sands missile range in the nearby desert are the reasons for most of the growth, and the Department of Defense is by far the largest employer. On its nonmilitary side, El Paso's economy is primarily based on trade and distribution. There are, however, some factories which exploit deposits of oil and copper a few hundred miles away (no great distance in the Southwest) and some which employ cheap labor from the slums of the city and from across the border. El Paso manufactures most of the world's blue jeans, but manufacturing is not a very important part of its economy.

The influx of soldiers, engineers, technicians, and supporting workers has stabilized the local economy—El Paso has no fear of widespread unemployment as long as the Cold War lasts—and it has brought unprecedented prosperity. Median family income was $5,211 in 1959, an increase of 68 per cent from 1949. Housing is good on the average and the rate of home ownership is high (58 per cent in 1960). About half the workers have white collar jobs.

The averages conceal much poverty, however, most of it among the Latins. In the South Side, a district of about 33,-000 Latins, almost 60 per cent of the housing is substandard and only 20 per cent is owner-occupied. The unemployment rate is high and the median family income low—less than $3,000 in 1959. But these averages are also deceiving. A sizeable Latin middle class is as well off as its Anglo counterpart and some of the Latins who live in the slums are recent arrivals from rural Mexico who will probably move on to better things after they have been in this country for a while. (El Pasoans think that *most* of the South Side residents are recent arrivals, but census figures show that this is far from being the case.)

Latins who can afford to do so may live in the best residential sections of the city. In El Paso (but nowhere else in Texas) there has never been "racial" discrimination against them. The city has never had a "Mexican" school; "high-class Mexicans" belong to the best clubs and intermarry with the best Anglo families. In recent years, however, there has been a marked growth of antipathy toward "low-class Mexicans"—that is, toward those who have not yet adopted middle-class ways.

About 15,000 Mexican nationals commute daily across the border from Juarez to work in El Paso. Their presence tends to keep wages down in the South Side and it probably obscures the economic and other progress that the Latins who have lived in the city for a long time have made. The arrival in recent years of so many defense workers has upset the numerical balance between Anglos and Latins: in 1950, Latins comprised more than two-thirds of the population; ten years later they comprised only about 45 per cent of it. The numbers do not tell the whole story, of course; the defense workers are mainly middle-class whites from the Northeast and the Midwest, and their presence is undoubtedly altering the cultural mix profoundly.

There are very few Negroes in El Paso (about 2 per cent of the population). Schools have been integrated and discrimination in theaters, restaurants, and hotels has been outlawed. Negroes of all social classes are nevertheless discriminated against in many ways.

How the Government Is Organized

El Paso elects a mayor and four aldermen (who together comprise the city council), two corporation court judges, an assessor and collector of taxes, and a treasurer for two-year terms in March of odd-numbered years. The charter gives the mayor authority to act as the city's chief executive, to prepare the budget, and to close saloons in case of riot. Technically the city has the strong-mayor-council form of government. In practice, however, the aldermen do not act together as a "board of directors"; instead by convention (not law) each is elected to a "place" which has the sole responsibility over some one set of functions. (Place 1, for example, supervises parks, recreation, and health.) The consequence is that general policy matters are rarely deliberated upon at all.

The mayor votes in council only to break a tie. He and the aldermen appoint more than 200 members of twenty-three boards, including the Plan Commission. The mayor appoints very few paid officials (city attorney and deputies, airport manager, clerk of courts) and these only with council approval. City employees are under a merit system which includes even the director of planning and the chief of police; the mayor can fire an employee only after a series of hearings. The city clerk, who is the city's general accountant, can refuse to sign checks if he thinks an expenditure improper. The mayor's authority to prepare the budget does not amount to much, for the council may alter it at will.

Water and sewage facilities are managed by a Public Service Board, an agency created to meet state requirements governing issuance of revenue bonds. Although the mayor is an *ex officio* member and the council has some say in the selection of the other members, the board is not only independent of the city government but sometimes works at cross purposes with it. Its critics say it is highly inefficient and much given to boondoggling.

The two school districts are run by independent, unpaid,

elected boards. Their payroll is considerably larger than that of the city.

Much authority is reserved to the electorate. State law requires referenda for most bond issues and tax increases, and in Texas it is common to refer controversial questions to a straw vote of the electorate even when the law does not require a vote.

How It Really Works

The mayor's ability to get things done depends more upon political skill and persuasiveness than upon the authority of his office. Some mayors have been highly effective, others almost entirely ineffective. A mayor cannot push an important measure through council unless he has been able to organize wide support for it first.

As a rule, mayors and aldermen are small businessmen who serve one or two terms from motives of public service. An alderman expects to spend about eight hours a week on city business. The mayor, however, is full-time (he is paid $9,600 plus $3,600 for expenses; aldermen get $4,800 plus $1,200 and are fined $5 for missing a council meeting without excuse), and this gives him a certain advantage over the aldermen. They may combine to oppose him, but as a rule they are not around city hall enough to originate serious proposals of their own.

Power is so widely distributed in El Paso that it is hard for the city government to undertake new programs. No one person or group has power enough to push anything through, and many can exercise what amounts to a veto. The slow-moving, relatively inactive city government that results seems to suit El Pasoans. They want their government to be a caretaker, not a builder or innovator. Homeowners complain if the Sanitation Department does not pick up tumbleweed fast enough, and they criticize the police for not catching more "teen-age vandals." But when they vote on bond issues, they show that they do not want new parks, libraries, or anything else that costs money; still less do they want their city government to be an active agent of social reform.

Several things help to account for these tastes. El Paso has a high rate of home ownership, and homeowners everywhere tend to oppose spending that would raise property taxes. Most voters live in suburban-type houses; they need fewer parks and other public facilities than apartment dwellers do. Furthermore ideological conservatism is strong in El Paso. Finally, the people who might be expected to want the most from an active city government—the poor Latins—are apathetic and politically ineffective.

How They Get Elected

Elections have been nonpartisan in El Paso since 1959, but the adoption of nonpartisanship did not significantly change local politics. Previously victory in the Democratic primary was tantamount to election; because all political battles were fought within it, the primary was in effect a nonpartisan election. Now elections are free-for-alls open to anyone willing to gamble a $100 filing fee. There are usually so many candidates for each office in the first (preliminary) election that none gets the majority needed for election; therefore a second (run-off) election is held between the two strongest candidates for each post.

Most serious candidates run on a "ticket" consisting of a mayoralty candidate and four council candidates. The city attorney ruled in 1963 that candidates on a ticket may not be listed together on the ballot, but running as part of a ticket has important advantages despite this limitation. Candidates united on a ticket can pool campaign funds, draw support from each other's friends and neighbors, present themselves as a "team," and offer a platform. Tickets are usually drawn up a few months before the election and generally melt away as soon as the votes are counted. The Peoples Ticket, however, has proved more durable, having appeared in four consecutive elections with some of the same candidates and the same base of support among poor and middle-class Latins. Even this ticket practically disappears between elections, however; unlike a party, it has no officials, headquarters, treasury, or full-time precinct workers.

On the poverty-stricken South Side, a small political ma-

chine operates. The "Organization," as it is called, consists
of ten to fifteen paid political workers (called *pistoleros* or
"gunslingers" by their South Side opponents) working under the direction of a boss. The Organization extends the
hand of friendship in the usual ways—it helps those in
trouble with the law, finds jobs, organizes clubs, holds rallies—and it expects the usual reward on election day for
having done so. Some say that the Organization is a profit-
making business and that anyone wishing votes on the
South Side can buy them from it for a fee of not less than
$1,000. Others doubt that it is for hire. Everyone seems to
agree, however, that it can sometimes be decisive in a primary, where the voters' lack of information about personalities and issues is greatest and the advice of the *pistoleros* is
most likely to be taken. In the nonpartisan city elections, the
Organization helps the Peoples Ticket by getting out a big
South Side vote. Apparently, however, it has no influence on
policy. "Politicians think their obligations to it end when
they pay it off," a politician told an interviewer.

In a run-off election, a wise candidate for mayor does not
spend much time campaigning among the poor Mexicans.
Those of them who have paid their poll taxes account for no
more than 15 per cent of the total vote. "It's better to go to
the shopping centers where the votes are than to mess
around the pool halls of the South Side," one experienced
Anglo said.

Not many people are actively involved in city campaigns.
Without job patronage or party loyalty to mobilize workers
during campaigns and to hold their interest between times,
there is no ready-made organization—except, of course, the
Organization—for a candidate to turn to. He must put together a volunteer organization as best he can, relying in the
main on relatives and friends. Sometimes an issue becomes
hot enough to bring enthusiasts to his headquarters; in recent years a good many Latins have been stirred up enough
by their political leaders to work hard in protest against
what they regard as the arrogance and indifference of the
Anglo majority. In an electoral system so unorganized, any
group with city-wide organization and money to spare is in
a highly advantageous position. In El Paso this means pri-

marily business groups. The newspapers also have more influence than they would if candidates carried party labels and had party backing.

ELECTIONS

In every election, the low-income, heavily "Latin" precincts in the southern part of the city along the Mexican border support one set of candidates and the well-to-do Anglo neighborhoods another. Precincts that are in-between economically and culturally are in-between politically as well, and the vote in these precincts is often decisive. In some (but not all) recent years the in-between precincts have tended toward the Latin side, that is, toward the Peoples Ticket.

The 1961 mayoralty campaign was fairly typical. A coalition formed around the Peoples Ticket included Latins, Negroes, the Organization, the *Herald-Post,* organized labor, and some small businessmen. On the other side were most "respectable" Anglos. Ralph E. Seitsinger, a furniture store owner who had served as an alderman, headed the Peoples Ticket. Julia Breck, the wife of a prominent physician, ran as an independent, without a ticket but with the support of many conservative Anglos. In the preliminary election there were four other candidates—three middle-class Anglos and one middle-class Latin. Seitsinger got 42 per cent of the vote and Mrs. Breck 24. In the run-off, these two fought for the votes that had been given to the lesser candidates. Seitsinger stressed his close personal association with the popular incumbent mayor, a Latin, promising to carry the mayor's policies forward. The issue before the electorate, he insisted, was whether the city should be governed by "all of the people or by the privileged few." Mrs. Breck emphasized "good government." El Paso's city administration, she said, was "inefficient" and "unbusinesslike"; moreover, the mayor was too much occupied with routine and "piddling." If elected, she would hire "qualified persons." (Many people thought this meant she would employ someone in a capacity like that of a city manager.) She made much of a charge that her opponent was obligated to "the machine" (the Organization). "Break the Machine with Breck" was her slogan.

Seitsinger won by 1,493 votes. Mrs. Breck got more than twice as many votes as in the preliminary election, in part because some middle-class Latins switched to her after the elimination of their preferred candidate. Seitsinger increased his vote too, but by only one-third. The huge lead he piled up in fifteen precincts controlled by the Organization, where he got 87 per cent of the vote, offset Mrs. Breck's advantage north of the tracks.

The People's victory was of brief duration. Seitsinger was able to accomplish little or nothing, and he provoked part of the electorate to fury by trying to enact a housing code (see page 78). In 1963 he finished third in the preliminary election; a "business conservative," the public relations man for a department store, succeeded him as mayor.

Interest Groups and Influentials

BUSINESS

Although the Latins often have the votes to elect a mayor, it is the businessmen who have the greatest influence in the conduct of affairs. One reason for this is that most of those elected to office in El Paso are themselves businessmen who believe, along with most middle-class El Pasoans, that "What's Good for El Paso Business Is Good for El Paso." Ordinarily, there is no need for the business community to bring any pressure on city hall: the elected officials do what the businessmen want without being asked. If need be, however, business can draw upon a stock of influence it wields as the biggest source of financial support in election campaigns. And if this were not enough, business has the advantage of being practically the only interest group in the city. Organized labor is weak. There are no strong civic associations, lack of interest and internal divisions make the Latin community particularly lacking in influence. The city's biggest newspaper, the *Times,* is on the side of the leading businessmen.

The businessmen have three organizations: the Chamber of Commerce, the Downtown Development Association, and the El Paso Industrial Council. The few most important

businessmen—"Kingmakers," they are sometimes called—
have no separate organization; they work through all three
business organizations, which they dominate.

The Kingmakers' most important goal is said to be keep-
ing the unions weak. The El Paso Industrial Council, labor
leaders say, is "strictly a strike-breaking outfit." Since so
many lines lead to Washington, there are, of course, decided
limits to what even Kingmakers do. They try, almost always
successfully, to keep those politicians who have particularly
close ties to the unions out of local office and to counteract
the influence of the unions with the politicians who are in
office. They also do what they can to see that officials have
the "right attitude" on assessments, tax rates, off-street park-
ing, highway location, traffic control, and similar matters.

Despite the great influence of the Kingmakers, El Paso's
business community is not monolithic. There are some Latin
businessmen who are often closer politically to the poor
South Side than to the Anglo interests. Some national corporations with branches in El Paso—Texaco and Phelps-
Dodge, for example—have come to terms with labor and
do not participate in the Industrial Council or in local politics. Sometimes, also, a split occurs among the Anglo businessmen, as when enactment of a housing code was proposed recently. Builders and real estate men favored the idea
and landlords opposed it.

LABOR

Organized labor has little influence in El Paso's politics, for
many reasons. The unions are poor and weak because of the
plentiful supply of cheap labor from Juarez, the Texas
"right to work" laws, and the militantly anti-union stand of
employers. Being poor and weak, the unions cannot mobilize precinct workers, persuade their members and supporters to pay poll taxes, or get big turn-outs on election day.
They are under other handicaps also. Many of their members have little or no interest in local politics, the local press
has been unfriendly, the Organization competes with them
for the allegiance of poor Latins, and many El Pasoans are
union-haters. Taking one thing with another, the best labor
can hope for from the city's politicians is to be ignored.

About 14,000 El Pasoans (12 to 15 per cent of the labor force) belong to seventy-five locals. The Central Labor Union represents about thirty-five of these, which include well over half El Paso's union members. Closely affiliated with the Central Labor Union (sharing the same office and the same director) is a recently organized chapter of the AFL-CIO Committee on Political Education (COPE). Before this came into being, labor's spasmodic political efforts were led by the Central Labor Union, its weekly *Labor Advocate,* and certain locals. These efforts were generally unsuccessful, and so far COPE's have not been much more so.

Evidences of labor's political weakness are easy to see. Labor leaders have no voice in the selection of city candidates (their choice, they say, is "to stay out of it altogether or else endorse the least of the evils running") and no representation on city boards. Contractors working for the city are not required to use union labor. Mayors who take up city problems with "community leaders" rarely include union men in the discussions. Nothing would please the Central Labor Union, AFL-CIO, more than to reduce the number of Mexican nationals commuting across the border. So far, however, it has had no success at all in this.

But city officials do not dare attack labor. By making themselves the advocates of the poor Latins, the unions make certain that no candidate will find it profitable to do so.

THE PRESS

El Paso has two daily newspapers. The locally-owned *Times* (daily circ. 56,341; Sunday, 78,071) is, like W. J. Hooten, its editor for more than twenty years, sober, circumspect, and conservative. It supports the interests of what it calls "El Paso's leading citizens" (for all practical purposes the "Kingmakers"), it has a booster spirit about local improvements, a go-slow spirit about integration, and a conservative outlook on state and national politics.

The evening *Herald-Post* (circ. 40,068), a Scripps-Howard paper, was edited for many years by a crotchety conservative who now and then supported Latins against certain Anglos he disliked. When he retired in 1962, his place was taken by a young man, Robert W. ("Pete") Lee, who has usually sided with the liberal and "enlightened" element of the community. Soon after his arrival in El Paso, Lee scored a political success by backing the winning candidate for mayor before the preliminary election had narrowed the field.

LATINS

El Paso was predominantly Latin until the 1950's. Many Latin families have lived in or near the city since the sixteenth century. About 12 per cent of the city's population was born in Mexico; the parents of another 30 per cent were born there. The Latins' influence is not in proportion to their numbers, however. Usually there is only one Latin on the city council and one on the school board. None of El Paso's five state representatives is a Latin. Only one mayor in recent history has been a Latin. Although their votes have often been decisive in city and county elections, the Latins have little to show for it.

One reason for the Latins' political incapacity is poverty. Another is lack of education. The rate of illiteracy among Latins is high; many cannot understand English, let alone speak or write it. But perhaps the Latins' most serious handicap is their persistent attachment to Mexican, rather then North American, cultural standards. Among other things, this leads them to be satisfied with things as they are. "We are too apathetic, too lethargic," one Latin told an interviewer. "The Mexican *peon* has never had much. He's better off in El Paso than he ever was in Mexico. Consequently, he's pretty content with things as they are." Along with this contentment goes a generalized distrust of government. ("The only thing most people in Mexico get from their government is trouble.") Either from contentment or mistrust, or both, Latins tend to steer clear of government and everything that pertains to it. Some 30,000 Latins in El Paso have not become American citizens; of those who have, thousands who could afford to pay their poll taxes have not done so. And of those who have paid their poll taxes, many do not vote.

Some say that prejudice on the part of Anglos is one of the main difficulties that Latins face in politics. The prejudiced Anglo, it is said, refuses to admit that any Latin is qualified for office and is apt to be obsessed with the notion that "Latins will take over everything if they get a chance." To this charge conservative Anglos reply, "Not so." The real trouble, they say, is that Latins are not used to democratic politics and cannot seem to learn how to play the game properly. A Latin politician, the Anglos say, has not the slightest comprehension that government should serve a *public* purpose; he assumes that his personal aggrandizement is all that matters and he stirs his followers to discontent and ill-will for no other purpose than to get himself into a position where he may apply the *mordido* ("bite"). Thus (according to this account) it is respect for the proper principles of good government, and not racial prejudice, that causes Anglos to favor Anglo candidates and oppose Latin ones.

Two organizations are trying to get Latins to take more interest in politics. The LULACS (League of United Latin American Citizens), a national group, has several El Paso chapters. It is nonpartisan and therefore does not endorse candidates; instead, it tries to increase Latin political activity by running poll tax drives and citizenship and English classes. The LULACS often speak for the Latins, especially in matters relating to education and housing. *Los Compadres* is an East El Paso neighborhood group that conducts extensive and effective door-to-door campaigns for candidates it endorses. Occasionally it takes neighborhood problems, such as poor street lighting or lack of parks, to city officials. PASO (Political Association of Spanish-speaking Organizations) is a regional group which was organized in San Antonio a few years ago to work for the nomination and election of "good" (that is, moderate and liberal) candidates. Its El Paso chapter is trying to set up a precinct-level organization in the Latin neighborhoods to "educate voters on important issues." It hopes in time to develop enough prestige and influence to be consulted on Latin appointments to public bodies.

Few middle-class Latins participate in these efforts. To

them politics is not a natural way of rising in the world. Most want to have nothing to do with it.

How Issues Are Handled

RACE

Sometimes El Paso's politics produces surprising results. The city was the first in Texas to integrate schools and the first to outlaw discrimination in restaurants, theaters, and hotels. This happened without much prodding from Negroes and with little opposition from whites. Businessmen were eager to make El Paso a convention city and they had tacit support from the Latins, who have always disliked racial discrimination. Besides, El Paso has very few Negroes.

URBAN RENEWAL

It is not always so easy to reach agreement. In 1962 Mayor Seitsinger proposed enactment of a housing code, partly in order to do something about the overcrowded, rundown, toiletless tenements on the South Side, but mainly to enable the city to qualify for federal urban renewal aid, specifically insurance of mortgages on low- and middle-income housing. Mortgage insurance, Seitsinger believed, would stimulate improvement in housing and would lead indirectly to reductions in the cost of fire and police protection and to greater tax revenues. A number of contractors and mortgage financiers agreed with the mayor and supported him; he had a political interest in improving housing, and they had a business one.

This alliance was opposed by another consisting of tenement owners and conservatives. Some of the conservatives were moderate. Mrs. Breck, the unsuccessful candidate for mayor the year before, favored a "locally controlled" housing code but feared "the heavy, heavy hand of the Federal government." Others, however, were extremist ideologues. ("The housing code idea sounds like something coming out of the Kremlin.") Seitsinger lumped the opponents together as "John Birchers and their fellow travelers." He assured the tenement owners that the code would be enforced "discreetly"—he could not, of course, tell them in so many words that its purpose was to enable the city to qualify for federal urban renewal aid—but this did not satisfy them. From their standpoint it was a bad thing to have a code on the books at all: a future mayor might enforce it even if Seitsinger did not; indeed, the Federal government might insist that it be enforced as a condition to further assistance, and if it were enforced, some owners of blighted properties would lose them. The tenement owners and the right-wing ideologues carried on a vehement campaign against the code through newspaper advertisements, some of which conveyed a hint that ladies' honor might not be entirely safe if a code were adopted. ("A city inspector will go around at night to inspect your sleeping area.")

None of this would probably have made much difference if the big downtown business interests and the newspapers had been enthusiastically in support of renewal. In fact, business opinion was mixed; some businessmen thought that it would be a good thing to stimulate construction of low-cost housing by the use of mortgage insurance; almost all, however, were conservative and anti-government as a matter of principle; besides, they hated to get in the middle of a fight. The newspapers were frankly disapproving. The *Times* did not condemn the proposed code, but it was clear that it did not like urban renewal. The *Herald-Post* said less on the subject, but what it did say was more sharply critical.

The city council's hearings on the code were tumultuous. Property owners filled the hall. They roared and hooted when right-wing ideologues lambasted the mayor, wept into microphones that America was falling under a dictatorship, and announced a movement to recall the mayor and the aldermen. Not all of the opponents of the code were crackpots, however. One of the most impassioned speakers at the hearings was a prominent lawyer, a supporter of Lyndon B. Johnson, whose identification was more liberal than conservative. After several weeks of frenzied hearings, Seitsinger and the aldermen jumped at a suggestion by the *Times* that the code be submitted to a referendum later. El Pasoans heaved a sigh of relief at the prospect of a return to civic sanity.

LOS ANGELES:

Pre (Civil) War

If it lived up to its national reputation, Los Angeles would have the newest of new-fangled city governments. In fact, it has a form of government that was considered obsolete half a century ago. Before the Civil War, most American cities had what Los Angeles has now—a mayor almost too weak to cut ribbons, a large elected council with administrative as well as legislative functions, and a great many more or less independent departments run by part-time boards of citizens. These arrangements, the work of reformers who wanted to put power out of the reach of "boodlers," were short-lived almost everywhere. For decades cities have been getting rid of their citizen boards, reducing their councils to an advisory and legislative role, and bringing the departments under the authority of the mayor. All except Los Angeles: although it is now the third largest city in the United States, with an annual municipal budget of about $500 million, its form of government is more or less what it started with. The Los Angeles political system *may* live up to the city's reputation, but not by being new-fangled.

Population and Economy

The city of Los Angeles is to be distinguished from Los Angeles County. The county consists of innumerable unincorporated places and seventy-four cities, of which Los Angeles city is one. The city sprawls over almost 458 square miles, 11 per cent of the area of the county. Unlike most cities, Los Angeles is not surrounded by its county; the two interpenetrate, fingers of each reaching many miles into the other. The population of the city was 2,479,015 in 1960, and that of the county 6,038,771.

Since 1925 the city's population has tripled. Natural increase and immigration do not account for all of the gain; the city has made more than 100 annexations. If its boundaries had not changed since 1850, when it was incorporated, Los Angeles' population would have declined slightly between 1950 and 1960. Actually it grew by 25.8 per cent and is still growing by about 40,000 persons a year.

Some of the annexed places have survived as "communities" within the city. Westwood, the site of the UCLA campus, is a community in this sense—that is, a locality to which many people feel more attached than they do to the city as a whole. There are also within the boundaries of Los Angeles some "communities" that are legal-political entities: the city of Beverly Hills, for example, is surrounded by the city of Los Angeles.

Because of the geographic interpenetration of city and county, the differences of income, class, and race between city and county populations are not very marked. The median family income in the city was $6,896 in 1959; in the county it was $7,046. In the city 33 per cent of the population is of foreign stock; in the county the percentage is 27.

The Negro population of the city has been increasing rapidly and is now about 14 per cent of the total. Negro settlement is spreading into the southern and western parts of the city. To find places to live, most Negroes have to buy homes and take in boarders. Mexican-Americans, the largest of the foreign-stock groups, comprise 5.6 per cent of the population; they live close to the Negro districts. Orientals, mostly Chinese and Japanese, comprise 3.1 per cent of the population and live in most parts of the city. Canadians and Russians are the other large foreign-stock groups. Most of the Russians are Jewish. About 325,000 Jews live in or near the city.

The economy is highly diversified. The largest industries are transportation equipment, aircraft, motion pictures, and building; however, food and food products, agriculture, fabricated metal products, petroleum, chemicals, wearing apparel, and machinery are also important. Los Angeles is the nation's third most important banking and financial center.

How the Government Is Organized

The principal elements of the city government are a mayor, a fifteen-member council, and nineteen independent board-run departments. The mayor is elected at large (along with a city comptroller and a city attorney) for a four-year term at a salary of $25,000. The councilmen are elected from districts for four-year overlapping terms and are paid $12,000. The members of most of the boards are appointed for five-year staggered terms by the mayor with the consent of the council; in most cases they are part-time and unpaid.

The charter, which runs to more than 300 pages, says that the mayor is "the executive officer of the city and shall exercise a careful supervision over all of its affairs." However, it also says that the council is "the governing body of the city" and that the boards are "to supervise, control, regulate, and manage" the departments. The mayor can do little besides make appointments and removals (without council approval he can appoint and remove only his own secretary), prepare a budget (which the council may change in any way by majority vote), and veto ordinances (the council can override his veto by a two-thirds or, in some matters, a three-fourths vote). The charter, the city attorney has ruled, does not give the mayor "any control over the officers and employees of the City."

The council is very powerful. It can not only add to and subtract from the mayor's budget, but, by majority vote, it can fix the salaries of employees, exempt certain employees from civil service provisions, decide planning and zoning questions, call elections, and place propositions, including charter amendments, on the ballot. It meets as a body five mornings a week and in committees most afternoons. The mayor is not its presiding officer; mayors rarely ask to appear before it and some have practically no face-to-face contact with council members.

A city administrator stands between the mayor and the council and is an adviser to both. He is appointed by the mayor and may be removed by the mayor with the consent of the council; the council itself, however, may remove him by a two-thirds vote.

Each part-time board, with one exception, appoints a general manager to administer its department. (The chief of police, for example, is responsible to a board.) The general managers can be removed only in accordance with civil service procedures; they therefore have a good deal of independence. Some departments control their own funds and are largely independent of the council.

Schools are run by a seven-member board of education, elected at large for four-year terms.

The county is governed by a five-man board of supervisors representing districts of about 1,000,000 persons. Under the "Lakewood Plan," it provides any or all of the usual local government services to such cities as contract for them. Los Angeles provides most services for itself.

Few matters are decided without first being referred to the electorate. Between 1925 and 1963, for example, 301 proposed charter amendments were submitted to the voters.

How It Really Works

In Los Angeles the extreme decentralization prescribed by law is not mitigated or overcome, as it is in some cities (Chicago, for example), by informal arrangements. The mayor is not a party boss and he has no patronage to distribute; if he is to have his way, it must be by persuasion or force of personality.

The councilmen are, of course, interested in the problems of their districts, not those of the city as a whole. The districts are big enough to be cities themselves (they range from 140,000 to 200,000 in population and up to 67 square miles in area). For the convenience of constituents, some of whom live so far from city hall that they would have to pay a toll charge to telephone it, most councilmen maintain a branch office staffed by a field secretary. A constituent who thinks the palm trees along the street need trimming, who is bothered by a barking dog, or who wants bigger storm drains, calls the councilman, who takes the matter up with the appropriate city department. "By custom," a councilman

said, "the councilman is considered the administrator of the
city services in his district." As much as 25 per cent of the
work of a district public works office, a recent check
showed, is done at the request of a councilman and without
any specific order from the board in charge of the department.

If a board does not like this arrangement, there is not
much that it can do about it. It is within the council's power
to give or withhold from the departments, and it always follows the rule of councilmanic courtesy—in matters affecting
his district, every councilman gets the automatic support of
all the others.

Every mayor has had frequent acrimonious fights with
the council, but most mayors eventually accept the inevitable and let the council and the departments run the government as they see fit. However, Mayor Samuel W. Yorty,
who took office in 1961, was determined to resolve both the
ambiguities and the silences of the charter in favor of the
powers of his office. This led to a ceaseless tooth-and-nail
struggle between him and the council. The council, Yorty
declared publicly, consists of "would-be ward bosses subser-
vient to powerful selfish interests." Early in his administration he proclaimed an end to "secrecy in government" and
set aside Wednesday mornings for a televised press conference at which he often made slashing attacks upon the
council. It responded by calling him names ("egomaniac,"
"paranoid," "would-be dictator"), making hash of his
budget (it cut hundreds of thousands of dollars in items that
he proposed and added millions in items of its own), eliminating the jobs of most of his staff, and pigeonholing whatever he proposed. When he began a weekly "Ask Your
Mayor" radio program, it demanded, and got, equal time for
an "Ask Your Councilman" broadcast.

The running battle between the mayor and the council
made miles of headlines, but it did not have much effect on
the conduct of routine city business. The council and the
departments continued as before jointly to manage matters
of interest to the districts, like rubbish collection and street
surfacing. Matters that were (or were supposed to be) of
city-wide concern—for example, fluoridation of water sup-

plies, urban renewal, civil defense, and planning for the city's further growth—for the most part continued, as before, to be ignored.

How They Get Elected

The mayor and eight members of the council are elected at the same time; the other councilmen are elected two years later. Elections are nonpartisan. A primary is held in April and a general election in May. In a mayoralty year about 42 per cent of the population votes in the primary and 49 per cent in the run-off; in other years the percentage voting in the primary is almost the same, but voting in the run-off is slightly less—about 42 per cent.

THE MAYORALTY ELECTION

To be a candidate for mayor one need only deposit a $500 bond and present a petition bearing 500 signatures. Usually there are many candidates, of whom only two or three are serious contenders. The leading contender is likely to have been hand-picked by the large downtown businesses, the manufacturing and utility companies, and the daily metropolitan press, especially the *Los Angeles Times*. When these interests have agreed upon a candidate, they hire a public relations firm to run his campaign. The firm is told what issues are important and what the budget is: the rest is up to it.

Neither party is well organized in Los Angeles, and—officially—both stay out of local politics. However, in some communities there are unofficial Democratic clubs, which sometimes provide energetic and skilled precinct workers to assist favored local candidates.

Normally an incumbent—particularly if he is supported by business and the metropolitan press—is assured of re-election. Upsets do occur, however. In 1961 Norris Poulson, the incumbent, had the support of all who "mattered," including business, press, the AFL-CIO, and, behind the scenes, the Republican party. Yorty had alienated the Democrats by supporting Nixon for president; his main supporter was a TV newscaster. In the primary Poulson came in

well ahead of the field, but in the general election Yorty won
by 276,000 to 260,000. His strategy was much like that two
other underdogs—Cavanagh in Detroit and Collins in Boston—were following at the same time. He relied heavily
upon TV appearances to convey an impression of his own
freshness, vigor, and sincerity and to convince his audience
that his heavily favored opponent was a tool of the "power
structure," which meant especially the *Times*. He also benefited from the belief, widely held among Negroes and Mexican-Americans, that he would replace the chief of police, a
man highly regarded among police professionals but considered unsympathetic by minority group leaders. (In fact, he
kept him.) In the 1965 primary Yorty defeated Representative James Roosevelt and six other candidates. He got 59
per cent of the total vote and therefore did not have to face
a run-off. More money was said to have been spent in the
primary than in any mayoralty race in the city's history. According to the *Los Angeles Newsletter,* Democratic campaign sources, like state-regulated banks and savings and
loan associations, stopped giving to Yorty as soon as it became clear that Roosevelt was in the race; Yorty's money
therefore came almost entirely from Republicans. The campaign was a clean one, and the voter turn-out, 58 per cent
of those registered, was the highest on record for a primary.

COUNCIL ELECTIONS

Council candidates depend mainly upon personal followings. Incumbents are able to build followings by "giving
service" (that is, "doing favors") for constituents, and
normally an incumbent who looks after his district is sure of
reelection. He may even get an absolute majority in the
primary, in which case he need not campaign further. Sometimes, however, a challenger arranges matters so as to divide
the incumbent's vote and defeat him.

Party connection and ideology do enter into council races
to some extent, however. "Although the parties as such
don't play any part in elections," a councilman said, "some
of the groups associated with them do. I am known as a
conservative Democrat, but I try to get support from both
sides—from Republicans as well as Democrats. The people

associated with the parties watch my record on city-wide issues. The ordinary voter, however, is more interested in having a fire station near him and in having his rubbish collected."

The usual way of getting into council politics is to work in a civic association. This makes one knowledgeable about a particular subject—taxation, for example—and also "known" in the district; it leads also to ties with the community press, local business groups, labor unions, and other civic associations. Eventually one may bring these groups together as a personal following. "I was active in youth work in my district until I reached the age of fifty-one," a councilman said. "Until I reached that age, I felt I couldn't afford to go into politics. (I had been in the banking and general contracting business.) When finally I figured I could afford it, I called in the people I had been working with on youth matters and asked for their support."

Normally a campaign for council costs about $15,000 to $20,000. Contributions come from interest groups within the district. Until 1964, when the legislature restricted the political activity of the employees of all local governments except school districts, city employees frequently contributed both money and services as campaign workers. Most candidates hire public relations firms to run their campaigns. These firms use most of the campaign funds to buy advertisements in the community press, posters, and—sometimes—leaflets making scurrilous, eleventh-hour charges against opponents. Council candidates do not buy TV time; that is too expensive a way to reach a district-size constituency.

Until recently the size of the districts and the scattered pattern of Negro residence kept Negroes off the council. Early in 1963, however, the council, to block another candidate favored by Mayor Yorty, filled a vacancy by appointing a Negro. A few months later, the Negro who had been appointed was elected along with two others.

Interest Groups and Influentials

BUSINESS

Ten years ago downtown business had a great deal of power
in Los Angeles affairs; now it has very little. ("The 'downtown power bloc' which once sent shivers down the backs of
local officials would probably now have trouble lobbying a
resolution in favor of Boy Scout Week through City Council," the *Los Angeles Newsletter,* a confidential weekly, remarked in its issue of July 18, 1964.) The principal reason
for the change seems to be the rapid growth and spread of
both the city and the metropolitan area: so many people
now live in outlying sections and in suburbs that downtown
no longer is important to politicians, or for that matter to
businessmen, whose interests now tend to be county-wide
and region-wide. The Los Angeles Chamber of Commerce,
one of the biggest and best-financed chambers in the country, is active in attracting new industry, promoting the
tourist trade, and securing economy and efficiency in government—but on a Southern California, not a central Los Angeles basis. Its influence with the mayor and council is accordingly small. The Downtown Business Men's Association
pushes urban renewal, mass transit, and other measures to
revitalize the business center, but its push is not very vigorous. A third business group, the Merchants' and Manufacturers' Association, is concerned primarily with labor relations; it was the principal proponent of a "right to work"
proposal that failed at the polls.

All three business groups probably come closest to exer-
cising influence when they sponsor or oppose referendum
proposals, an activity which takes money. The Chamber of
Commerce, for example, has a better chance of reducing
taxes by trying to defeat an expenditure proposal on the
ballot than by nagging officials (the voter, after all, is the
one who decides in Los Angeles). Even so, the Chamber's
chance is not very good: most such business crusades fail.

THE PRESS

The morning *Los Angeles Times* (daily circ. 768,503; Sunday 1,094,990) is one of the most profitable newspapers in the country. (It carries more advertising than any other paper in the world.) Its publisher is Otis Chandler, the thirty-six-year-old (in 1964) son of Norman Chandler, chairman and president of the Times Mirror Company, about half the $177 million income of which comes from newspaper operations. The evening *Herald-Examiner* (daily circ. 713,318; Sunday 718,811) is a Hearst paper. Both Los Angeles papers are vehemently conservative. Their endorsement, especially that of the *Times*, is believed to count for a great deal with a substantial part of the electorate. Many voters, however, are automatically distrustful of any politician who is warmly supported by the daily press. Poulson's defeat by Yorty was largely a revolt against the *Times*, which had long exercised an almost proprietary influence at city hall. "We love our city and we weep for it," the *Times* said when the returns were in. Some of the tears, perhaps, were for its own loss of influence.

LABOR

Union leaders call Los Angeles a "tough" town. Membership there is relatively small, and no one union dominates the labor movement. Not since 1911 has labor come close to controlling the city politically, and even then it was frustrated by the involvement of two labor leaders in the bombing of the *Times*. The unions have since stuck closely to "bread and butter" matters, although they have expressed themselves now and then on public housing, rent control, and the municipal ownership of water and power utilities. A labor-led Voters League sometimes participated in election campaigns, apparently with little effect. The *Times* is bitterly anti-labor.

NEGROES

Despite the large numbers of Negroes, Orientals, Mexicans, and Jews in the electorate, Los Angeles politics was until very recently monopolized by white Protestants. The Los

Angeles branch of the NAACP had only about 8,000 members in 1960—too few to support even a single staff man. (The Urban League had a staff of five, but it was supported from the Comunity Chest and did little but try to find jobs for Negroes.) In the spring of 1963, however, not one but three Negroes were elected to the council. At the same time, Dr. Martin Luther King surprised and impressed the city by drawing 30,000 people to a Wrigley Field rally. CORE also appeared upon the scene and engaged the school board in a bitter, pointless row over *de facto* segregation (pointless because the school board was doing what little it could do to improve the situation). In the spring of 1964 a United Civil Rights Committee sponsored a mass demonstration and a rally in the Sports Arena, one purpose of which was to raise funds for the NAACP. Negro militants in a political action group, the Democratic Minority Conference, have fostered the organization of Democratic clubs in the heavily Negro and Mexican districts in order to increase their weight in the Democratic state organization. DMC makes a frankly racist appeal; it refuses membership to Caucasians, including Jews, but accepts Mexicans (apparently it thinks that Mexicans are not Caucasians). These and other efforts to form a political alliance between Negroes and Mexicans seem to have had little success.

Los Angeles has four Negro newspapers. The largest, the *Sentinel,* has a circulation of about 25,000.

How Issues Are Handled

Los Angeles does not have a mass transit system, it does not fluoridate its water, its public housing program is dead, and its urban renewal program is moribund. As this suggests, city-wide programs that are at all controversial have tough going in Los Angeles. One reason is that the only elected official having city-wide responsibility for such matters—the mayor—is nearly powerless. Another is that the fragmentation of authority is so great as to make almost any action difficult. Even in the unlikely event that the mayor, the council, and the independent boards all agree, a proposed undertaking still has other hazards to face. The agreement of the county Board of Supervisors may be needed (the Supervisors are very much involved in the mass transit question, for example). So is that of the voters, for almost everything has to be passed on in a referendum. Finally a last-ditch stand may be made in the courts. The wonder is that anything at all gets done.

If one asks why the city does not centralize authority, the answer is that structural reform is subject to all of the normal difficulties in the way of getting anything done and more besides. Since 1924, when the present charter was adopted, there have been repeated efforts to replace it. Dozens of official and unofficial bodies have made studies and offered recommendations favoring the strong-mayor-council form of organization that most large cities have long had. None of these efforts at fundamental reorganization has come anywhere near success.

Mayor Yorty stirred up a new effort at reform soon after he took office. A men's civic association, Town Hall, hired a professional expert to make a study and then (in 1963) issued an elaborate report calling for a strong mayor and a part-time council, two-thirds of whose members would be elected at large. Had it been disposed to, the council could have put a charter amendment along these lines on the ballot. But it would never put any proposal on the ballot that might lead to a reduction of its own power or to a gain in the power of the mayor, and therefore it ignored the Town Hall report, as it had other reports by similar bodies before.

Without the council's cooperation, the road to reorganization is hard. To put on the ballot a call for the election of a board of freeholders (a body which would draft a new charter for submission to the voters) it is necessary to get up a petition signed by about 200,000 registered voters within a six-month period. The civic associations are not able to do this: Town Hall, for example, is a study and discussion forum, not a political organization. If business interests had enough at stake, they might put up the $100,000 that would be necessary to hire a commercial agency to collect the signatures. (The going rate is 50 cents a signature.) A good many businesses would like to see the city government strengthened. They are not likely to spend so much money, however, simply to get a call for a board of freeholders on the ballot.

The newspapers—especially the *Times*—could help if they would. Along with the mayor, the metropolitan press is the only institution in a position to take a comprehensive view of city problems. But the press—especially the *Times* —enjoys an unusual influence precisely because the mayor is weak, and, like the council, it is not likely to give this influence up. Besides, none of the newspapers—least of all the *Times*—wants to give aid or comfort to Mayor Yorty. Therefore they are not likely to take the initiative, and if they support a proposal for reform at all, their support will probably be lukewarm.

Yorty would have liked to have had a charter amendment reorganizing the city government on the ballot with him in 1965. The cost of getting it there—an estimated $100,000 or the equivalent in volunteer work—was more than he could safely spare from his own campaign, however. After his primary victory he said that if he could not get a board of freeholders elected to rewrite the charter he might appoint a commission to recommend changes. Either way it would not be easy to get the issue before the voters, and there was always the chance that in the end they might turn his proposal down.

Meanwhile, Yorty has made some progress toward his goal of strengthening the mayor's office by following other routes. He has assumed responsibility in matters concerning which the charter is silent. For example, he issued an executive directive which had the effect of centralizing all electronic data systems. This move led eventually to the passage by the council of an ordinance setting up a separate agency, the Data Service Bureau, to administer information systems. This was bound to have a centralizing effect; as one of the mayor's assistants put it, it "tied together the blood systems of twenty-five separate bureaucratic organisms." The mayor took another step in the same direction when he established the Youth Opportunities Board to deal with problems of welfare and delinquency prevention. The board cut across five major jurisdictional lines; the nature and urgency of the problems it was to deal with were such, however, that the affected jurisdictions accepted the arrangement willingly. By administrative measures of this sort, Yorty may strengthen the executive power somewhat and at the same time establish precedents which future mayors will use if charter revision proves impossible. Los Angeles may be making haste slowly, but it is pretty sure to get there in the end.

MIAMI (DADE COUNTY):

Yes, But . . .

For more than half a century, public administration people all over the United States have argued for the creation of general-purpose governments with jurisdiction over whole metropolitan areas. Efforts to establish metropolitan governments ("metros") failed everywhere until 1957, when the voters of Dade County, Florida (Miami and environs) accepted one. The Dade County voters have been going back to the voting booths at frequent intervals ever since to reconsider their decision. Their "Metro" (that is, the reorganized government of Dade County) seems at last to have taken a firm hold on life, but it will be a decade or two before it grows out of its infancy. Even so, the Miami area is likely to reach the goal recommended by the public administration experts ahead of any other big city in this country.

Until 1964 it was far from certain that Metro would survive, and even by then it had not lived up to its name or fame. All twenty-six cities within Dade County still operated more or less as they did before Metro came into existence: each city had its own police and fire department, its own parks and playgrounds, and its own housing program, water supply, and sewage disposal system. Each levied and collected its own taxes. Metro regulated traffic, collected the county-wide tax, provided some services to unincorporated areas of the county (although not all that it was supposed to provide), and had developed a seaport. The framework for a true metropolitan government is all there, however, and it is just a matter of time before one is created. Time—and also politics.

Population and Economy

Dade County is booming. Its population (935,047 in 1960) has almost tripled since the end of World War II. New settlers, attracted by the weather and the beaches, keep pouring into Greater Miami from all over the United States. The newcomers are making the unincorporated parts of the county grow fastest: the population of these areas tripled between 1950 and 1960, and they now have 38 per cent of the total. Another 31 per cent (291,688 persons) live in Miami; the rest is scattered among twenty-five other municipalities ranging in size from Indian Creek, with only 60 inhabitants, to Hialeah, with 66,972.

Hialeah is a predominantly working-class city. The next largest suburb is Miami Beach (pop. 63,145), a high-income tourist resort, with Coral Gables (pop. 34,793), an upper-income residential city and the site of the University of Miami, coming third. The residents of some cities are very proud of their local governments and tend therefore to be hostile toward Metro, which they regard as a competing, "outside" force. These local loyalties are one reason why Metro has not been able to exercise more of the powers given it in its charter.

Almost half of Dade County's workers are employed in distributive and service industries, many of which—aircraft operation and maintenance, wholesale and retail trade, and hotels and restaurants, for example—are tourist-oriented. The county's booming population growth has fostered a vigorous construction and real estate industry. Almost 60 per cent of the residents of Greater Miami own their homes. The Florida constitution encourages home ownership by giving a $5,000 tax exemption on the assessed value of every owner-occupied house.

There were 137,300 Negroes in the county in 1960; this was not quite 15 per cent of its population. Most of the Negroes are common laborers. About half live in three districts of Miami.

There is also a large Latin-American colony. Immigration is easy for Latin Americans who are both literate and finan-

cially responsible (that is, who have either a sponsor in this
country or at least $2,000 in a bank here), and at least 85,-
000 Latin Americans have settled in Miami and its environs.
After Castro's rise to power, they were joined by about
100,000 Cuban refugees. There are also many Puerto Ri-
cans. So far, no serious antagonisms have developed among
these groups or between them and the rest of the population.

It was estimated in 1958 that about 80,000 Jews live in
the Greater Miami area, three-fourths of them in Miami
and Miami Beach. The prevalence of Jews in Miami Beach
—they constitute well over half its population—makes it
the most liberal city in the county. Catholics number about
187,000, slightly more than 20 per cent of the county's population.

How the Government Is Organized

THE COUNTY COMMISSION

The "legislative and governing body of the county" is a
board of nine part-time commissioners, paid $6,000 a year.
Eight of the commissioners must be residents of different
districts, but they and the board chairman, called the "county
mayor," are elected at large in a county-wide vote. This plan
is the effect of a 1964 reorganization, which strengthened
the commission. Originally there were thirteen commissioners, five elected at large, five representing various districts,
and three representing the cities of Miami, Hialeah, and
Miami Beach.

The commission's ordinance-passing powers are great in
contrast with those of other Florida counties, which must
get a special act passed by the state legislature to make even
the most minor changes. Special acts set salaries for officials
and employees, supervise civil service, and decide how taxes
will be spent. The Metro commission has the same law-
making power as the state legislature over unincorporated
areas of Dade County, with one major exception: the legislature in Tallahassee still has the all-important taxing
power. Metro has no authority to enact new taxes.

Traffic regulation and prosecution of violators is now handled by Metro. City Traffic courts have been abolished. A citation issued by a municipal police officer is processed through Metro's traffic court.

The Metro commission also operates a county-wide bus system. It regulates service and rates for all privately-owned utilities within the county, including those inside city boundaries. It is building 200 miles of expressway, operates Miami International Airport, and has joined with the City of Miami to build a $20-million seaport. Beginning in 1964, all Metro invitations to bid on constant-supply items included a provision by which the successful bidder agreed to sell at the same price to any municipality. The charter requires all cities to adopt Metro's property assessment roll by 1966, so that assessing for tax purposes will then be completely consolidated.

THE COUNTY MANAGER

A professional county manager, appointed by the commission, receives a salary set at $30,000 by the commissioners, and is, according to the charter, "responsible to the Board of County Commissioners for the administration of all units of the county government under his jurisdiction, and for carrying out policies adopted by the Board." Subject to civil service rules, he has power to appoint and remove all administrative officers and employees. A series of conflicts between Metro's first manager, who tried to centralize county departments under his control, and the commissioners and other county officials who wanted to retain their influence resulted in charter amendments, approved by the voters in 1962, prohibiting the manager from appointing major department heads without approval from the commissioners. Metro's charter attempted to separate "politics," which is the commissioners' affair, from "administration," which is the manager's. To keep the commissioners from interfering with "administration," the charter requires that they deal with county officials only through the manager. It also prohibits them from appointing or removing county employees.

CITIES

Metro's charter provides that any city may be abolished and
its functions performed by Metro if—and only if—a majority of its voters consent. So long as it exists, a city exercises
"all powers relating to its local affairs not inconsistent with
the Metro charter." No cities have been abolished, and, with
the minor exceptions noted above, none has had any of its
functions taken over. Metro is waiting for the time to be
ripe. It wants to be sure of overwhelming support in the
cities to be affected, and it wants to perfect its present operations before undertaking new ones.

OTHER COUNTY OFFICES

The Metro charter made the offices of county sheriff and tax
assessor appointive. In November, 1963, the voters adopted
an amendment putting the sheriff's office back on the ballot.
(At the same time, however, they refused to do the same
thing with the tax assessor's.) Now the sheriff can be removed only by the governor.

County judicial offices—judges, justices of the peace,
clerks of court, and constables—are elected on a partisan
basis, as they are elsewhere in Florida.

SCHOOLS

An independent county Board of Public Instruction, with
authority to tax and to borrow, runs the public schools. It
has seven members elected at large in partisan elections.

How It Really Works

There has been a continuing struggle between the manager and the commissioners, with the other county officials
as their allies, to decide who would run Metro. The struggle
began when the first manager, O. W. Campbell, tried to
bring under his control a hodge-podge of departments that
reported to individual commissioners or to other elected or
appointed officials. His most difficult problem was with
certain officials who had previously been elected but were
now appointed—the sheriff, tax assessors, tax collector, and

surveyor. The charter had frozen the elected incumbents into these positions.

To strengthen his hand in dealing with the departments, Campbell created a budget office which functioned as a bureau of executive management. Administrative analysts from the budget office surveyed departmental operations and made recommendations for their improvement. For example, insurance was to be bought by competitive bid rather than from a few favored companies. Such improvements did not endear Campbell or his budget office to the old hands who had been running things before he appeared upon the scene. Eventually, however, he managed to reduce the number of departments and to establish control over them.

Campbell also fought the commissioners. To begin with, the county board consisted of five commissioners who had been elected under the old, pre-Metro county government. Some say that these commissioners resented their loss of power (formerly they had been able to make appointments and to award contracts) and were determined that Metro should not succeed. The commissioners themselves complained that Campbell did not keep them informed and failed to provide leadership. Whatever the reasons, Campbell and his board were frequently at odds. Nor did relations improve when six new commissioners were added. Finally, in 1961, with only one of its thirteen members dissenting, the board fired him.

It then hired Irving C. McNayr, who had been city manager of Columbia, South Carolina. He was more public relations-minded than Campbell had been, and in 1962, when some charter amendments which would have restricted his authority were put before the voters, he campaigned actively against them. He lost, however; the voters gave the board the right to approve his appointments to the position of department head as well as any administrative order he might issue creating or merging departments. Angered when the commissioners objected to his electioneering and angered also, presumably, by the outcome of the vote, McNayr resigned. He soon changed his mind, however. His differences with the commissioners were settled by an agreement that he would make public statements only on matters on which the commission had made policy decisions and that the commission would inform him of the majority view on all proposed charter amendments. He came in conflict with the commission again, however, when he urged consolidating the cities with the county. This idea drew criticism from all sides, and McNayr took a vow of silence. He broke his vow in 1964 by stumping the county (unsuccessfully) in opposition to a charter amendment which in effect took Metro's urban renewal powers away from it. Later that year, after a court ordered the doubling of tax assessments, the commission decided that McNayr had lost his effectiveness and unanimously asked for his resignation. He was succeeded in May, 1965, by Porter W. Homer, who had been the city manager of Rochester, N.Y.

How They Get Elected

Metro elections are held in May of even-numbered years. Although candidates for the Board of Commissioners run on a nonpartisan basis, the election is held at the same time as the party primaries. Two elections are usually necessary. If a candidate wins a majority in a primary, he is elected, otherwise—and this is the usual case—the two highest vote-getters run against each other in a second primary held three weeks after the first. There is no subsequent general election.

In putting elections for the Board of Commissioners on a nonpartisan basis, the Metro charter did not change matters fundamentally, for party affiliation had never been very important. Almost all candidates had run as Democrats. Because almost everyone wore the same party label, the real battles had been fought in the Democratic primary: in effect it had been a nonpartisan election.

The Dade County Democratic executive committee does not nominate or endorse primary candidates. Its sole function is to assist Democrats in general elections, a task made easy by the weakness of the local Republican party. The committee has little to say in the allocation of the 200 to 300 state patronage jobs that go to Dade County. These and other jobs are filled on recommendations from the *ad hoc* campaign groups which have supported the successful state candidates. Despite Eisenhower's overwhelming victories in Dade County, Republicans there have had little success in building a party organization or in getting out the vote. Cynics say that Republican leaders do not want an effective organization because it would mean less federal patronage for them.

Lacking help from an effective party organization, pre-Metro county officials used patronage, contracts, and personal charm to build political followings. Some had followings that kept them constantly in office for twenty years or more. Under Metro, the jobs and contracts are distributed by the manager, and commissioners' followings have shrunk accordingly. To win county office now, a candidate needs support from the Miami *Herald* and the Miami *News*. Endorsement by both newspapers almost assures victory. Support from prestigious persons, including local politicians and business and professional leaders, also helps. Campaign organizations—loose, temporary coalitions of more or less influential backers—usually form around candidates on an *ad hoc* basis.

Along with endorsements, money plays an important part in Metro campaigns. Incumbents and candidates supported by the newspapers can usually raise the largest war chests, because they are the candidates most likely to win. County-wide candidates usually feel that they must purchase TV time, and they also spend heavily for advertisements in the two metropolitan dailies. In 1964, the highest-spending candidates reported expenditures close to $30,000.

All candidates employ a "person-to-person" approach, ringing doorbells, visiting supermarkets and factories, shaking hands, and telling jokes. Before Metro there was little movement from city to county office; county commissioners usually were elected again and again. Now city officials are using their local followings to help them in Metro campaigns.

Interest Groups and Influentials

BUSINESS

The business community of Greater Miami consists chiefly of hotel owners, real estate and insurance brokers, public utility executives, department store owners, and manufacturers. The Miami-Dade Chamber of Commerce, although composed mainly of business and professional people in Miami, regards itself as a county-wide organization and is the only organization that speaks for business on all sorts of metropolitan affairs. It presents its views at meetings of the Miami and Metro commissions, it sponsors preelection radio-TV programs on which candidates answer questions, and it directed a successful campaign for an expressway bond issue. On the issue of Metro, its membership has been somewhat divided, although differences of opinion are kept within the organization. The downtown department stores, the daily newspapers (the chamber's ties with them are very close), and the manufacturing interests have always been among Metro's most ardent supporters. Firms doing business with the cities have been allied with the Florida Power and Light Company against Metro. An in-between group favoring gradual evolution of a federal system seems to have held the balance of power. The biggest bone of contention has been the status of the city of Miami: the consolidationists want to eliminate it.

When in 1959 a Miami University professor asked community leaders what organizations they thought had most influence on Metro's policies, the chamber got the most votes—108. The also-rans were the Dade League of Municipalities with 41; the Miami *Herald* with 40; the Miami *News* with 22; the University of Miami with 15; and station WTVJ with 13.

THE PRESS

In the absence of strong, cohesive parties and interest groups, the daily press has unusual influence in Miami. The morning *Herald* (daily circ. 302,756; Sunday 361,578) and the evening *News* (daily circ. 118,610; Sunday 115,531) have the same ownership. The *Herald* has played an active part in rallying the "good government" forces behind Metro, with which, accordingly, it has much influence. In the poll mentioned above, the *Herald's* political editor was mentioned almost as many times as the county manager in answer to the question: who has most influence in the affairs of Metro? The *Herald* succeeded in a campaign to have all county commissioners elected at large; this, of course, will give it even more influence.

There are twenty suburban and ethnic papers. These carry little news or editorial matter and do not have much political weight. The local Negro newspaper, the weekly Miami *Times,* neither endorses candidates nor editorializes on controversial issues. The most widely read Negro paper is the Pittsburgh *Courier,* which has a Miami edition.

LABOR

There are 50,000 union members in Dade County, but unions are not a significant force in local politics. The only locals that are active in local affairs are those with a direct interest in some particular issue, and the influence of these is usually nil. In elections, labor is on the winning side only when its endorsements coincide with those of the *Herald* or *News.*

Labor is frequently divided over endorsements. The Dade Federation of Labor, composed of some seventy locals, endorses candidates through its fourteen-member Committee on Political Education (COPE). This meets with the candidates, evaluates their replies to a questionnaire, and then makes recommendations to the Federation, which either accepts them by a two-thirds vote or else chooses other candidates for endorsement. Some locals, however, make their own endorsements, and often these do not coincide with those made by the Federation. Among the unions that most often take independent action are the Communications Workers, Longshoremen, Teamsters, and Hotel Employees.

MINORITY GROUPS

Minority groups and transplanted Northerners have an effect on Dade County politics. For one thing, they tend to keep the county isolated from the rest of the state. The badly apportioned state legislature, which is run by a "Pork Chop Gang" of rural county "rednecks," has always regarded Dade as a foreign land. The presence there of so many Jews and Yankees who are strongly sympathetic to the Negro puts the rural legislator on guard against it. In North Florida, the ultra-right thinks Metro is the next thing to Communism.

Dade County Negroes are in fact somewhat better off than other Southern Negroes. The county's public schools were the first in the state to be integrated. In the 1963-64 school year about one-fourth of them were integrated; 18 per cent of the Negro children attended predominantly white schools. The junior college, with five Negro faculty members, has for some time been the most integrated institution of higher learning in the South. All public recreational facilities are integrated. Most downtown hotels and restaurants serve Negroes, and almost all of Miami Beach's resort attractions are open to them. There is still almost total segregation in housing areas, however.

Until the early 1960's the Negro community had never been a factor in elections. But the 1964 spring primary, in which a candidate for governor from Miami was the sole supporter of the civil rights bill then pending in Congress, brought out an impressive Negro bloc vote.

The Miami area has no Negro college, and accordingly its Negro leaders are mostly clergymen rather than educators. The Negro Ministerial Alliance, composed of more than half the seventy-five Negro ministers in the area, is active in civil rights, in getting Negroes to register and vote (in 1960, only 20 per cent of the Negro population, as against 47.8 per cent of the white, was registered), and in crusading against gambling and vice. The president of the South Florida chapter of the NAACP, a minister, is a militant crusader for Negro rights.

There are many more Latin Americans in Dade County than Negroes. But not many of the Latin Americans (practically none of the Cuban refugees) are citizens, and probably fewer than 5,000 actually vote. The Federation of Hispanic-American Organizations of Dade County is attempting to create the impression that there exists a cohesive Latin voting bloc. So far it has not had any success at the polls.

The Jewish minority is politically powerful. It finds an issue of interest to it in almost every election and its members vote together. There is little discrimination in business or politics against Jews. Being Jewish or Catholic does not affect a candidate's chances for county-wide office, but a gentile might have problems running for office in the City of Miami Beach. There is social discrimination. The Anti-Defamation League complains of "5 o'clock shadow," meaning that contacts between Jews and non-Jews stop at the end of the business day.

How Issues Are Handled

The biggest issue in Dade County has long been Metro itself. It has been under constant attack. A rain of blows has been struck at it in the courts (it is sued about once a day); others have been struck through the charter-amending process. The first big test at the polls came in 1958, when Metro was still brand new. It tried to exercise jurisdiction over zoning and building codes, auto inspection, and traffic regulation, and the League of Municipalities responded by putting on the ballot an "autonomy" amendment which would have stripped it of many of its powers. The voters turned the amendment down by a margin of 3 to 2. Three years later, Metro fought off another attack. This time the voters were asked to eliminate its control over sewage, water supply, transportation, traffic, and central planning; to abolish the office of county manager; to reduce the number of commissioners to five; to make the office of sheriff elective; and to abolish the Metro traffic court. They refused by a margin of about 2 to 1. In November, 1963, the voters accepted some and rejected other proposed changes in the structure of the government (these were described above). Metro's powers were kept intact, however, and the charter-amending process itself was rendered a less useful weapon against it; whereas previously only about 14,000 signatures had been needed to get a proposed amendment on the bal-

lot, now about 41,000 (10 per cent of the electorate) would
be necessary. This did not end the spate of proposed amendments, however. In the spring of 1964 one was passed limit-
ing Metro's urban renewal process to unincorporated areas,
which is to say areas with nothing to renew.

The initiative for these attacks has come mostly from the
League of Municipalities, certain city officials, and county
officials whose positions were elective and are now appointive. These interests have been supported at the polls mainly
by tax-conscious homeowners. Metro was sold to the public
as a way of promoting efficiency and economy, but its
budget zoomed from about $38 million in 1957 to almost
$60 million in 1961. Although the budget leveled off then
and there were token tax decreases every year afterward, tax-
minded people are still alarmed, and the passage of the
urban renewal charter amendment in 1964 reflected their
hostility. The fight for the amendment was led by an attorney for the League of Municipalities, a former county legislator, who argued that voters living elsewhere should not
have to pay for urban renewal in Miami.

If voters outside Miami are afraid that Metro will favor
it, those inside Miami are afraid that it will not do enough
for them. Miami had most of its capital investments paid
for before Metro came along, and its residents tend to feel
that their city can do the job better and cheaper than Metro.
Since they have a big share of the voting strength in the
county, what they think is important. Until Metro is well
past the period of high initial costs from getting new programs under way, its standing in Miami will be somewhat
precarious. There is little doubt, however, that the city governments, Metro's principal opponents, are ready to come to
terms with it. They have established their main point, which
is that it must keep its hands off their most cherished functions. And Metro for its part has shown that it can keep the
support of the *Herald,* the Miami-Dade Chamber of Commerce, and the prosperous, "good government"-minded
middle class, and that, with this support, it can almost always get at least 50 per cent of the vote in a referendum.
Metro will probably lose some more battles, but it seems to
have won the war.

PHILADELPHIA:

Nice While It Lasted

Reform has put political machines out of business almost everywhere. Philadelphia is an exception, however; there a machine recently put reform out of business. A well-oiled Republican machine ran the city for 68 years until 1951. Then reform, in the persons of Joseph S. Clark, Jr., and Richardson Dilworth, both scions of aristocratic families, knocked the machine to pieces. A few years later, Congressman William J. Green, Jr., a saloonkeeper's son, used some of the remnants of the old Republican machine to build a new and powerful Democratic one. When he died (December 21, 1963), the reformers tried to gain control of the party. So far they have failed, but factional struggles have been breaking out in the Democratic ranks and Republican strength is said to be reviving. Eventually reform is likely to return as a dark horse.

Population and Economy

The persistence in Philadelphia of machine politics (meaning party politics based largely on jobs and favors rather than on interest in issues or personalities) is to be explained in part by the composition of the electorate. Middle-class whites, who tend to vote Republican and to favor "good government," have been moving out of the city to the suburbs; their places have been taken mainly by lower-class Negroes. Between 1950 and 1960 more than 200,000 whites left. At the same time, the nonwhite population increased from 18.2 per cent to 26.7 per cent. This left a total population of 2,002,512, 3.3 per cent less than in 1950. The movement of Negroes into Philadelphia is expected to continue. Some think that by 1980 the Negro population will reach 1,000,000.

Nearly 30 per cent of the city's population is of foreign stock. The two most numerous groups are Italian and Russian-Jewish; other large groups are English, Irish, Polish, German, and Puerto Rican. There are 256,000 Jews in Philadelphia, according to a 1957 survey by the Federation of Jewish Agencies. The Catholic population is probably 700,000 (including about 50,000 nonwhite Catholics), and the white Protestant population about 600,000.

Philadelphia has a highly diversified economy, with a combination of commerce and manufacturing and a good deal of variety within each category. It is a major seaport, ranking second to New York in tonnage. The leading industries are textiles, apparel, primary and fabricated metals, and machinery. Of employed persons in the city, 40.8 per cent are in white collar occupations and 33.2 per cent in manufacturing. The median family income in 1959 was $5,782, fifteenth among the nation's twenty-five biggest cities.

Philadelphia is a city of homeowners. In 1960, 61.9 per cent of the dwelling units were owner-occupied, more than in any other large city. All but 64,028 of the owner-occupied dwelling units were occupied by whites.

How the Government Is Organized

Under a home-rule charter adopted in 1951, Philadelphia is governed by a strong mayor and a seventeen-member city council. Both the mayor and the council are elected on a partisan basis. The mayor, whose term is four years, has unusual control over finances. He submits budget requests for all departments, boards, and commissions to the council and during the course of the year may reduce council appropriations for any department in order to avoid a deficit.

The mayor also has unusual power over appointments. The charter gives him four powerful aides: a managing director (who with the mayor's consent appoints the heads of the ten service departments and exercises general supervision over them), a director of finance (who is in charge of accounting and the preparation of the annual operating budget), a personnel director, and a city representative (who makes public appearances on behalf of the mayor). The personnel director is appointed by the Civil Service Commission (which in turn is appointed by the mayor from a list of nominees submitted by a panel of civic leaders), and the director of finance is appointed by the mayor from a list of nominees submitted by another panel. A city solicitor is appointed by the mayor with the consent of the council. Almost all other appointments are made by the mayor alone. A district attorney and a city controller are elected for four-year terms.

The new charter established a comprehensive merit system and banned political activity by city employees. It also limited the mayor to two terms of office.

The council is elected at the same time as the mayor. Seven of its members are elected at large; each party may nominate only five men for these places, an arrangement that assures the minority party of at least two seats. The council has broad legislative powers: it can enter any field that the legislature has not specifically reserved for itself. It has no administrative authority.

SCHOOLS

City and school affairs are entirely separate both in theory and in fact. Legally the school district is governed by an unpaid fifteen-member Board of Education appointed by the judges of the Courts of Common Pleas for overlapping, six-year terms. In fact, a school superintendent and a business manager, both employed by the Board, run the system and, some say, the Board as well.

THE COUNTY

When the legislature authorized the new home-rule charter for Philadelphia, it also passed a city-county consolidation act. Since 1854 the city and county had had identical jurisdictions. The changes brought all but some minor quasi-judicial offices into the city government.

How It Really Works

Despite the merit system provisions of the charter, the mayor controls several hundred patronage jobs which, together with the considerable formal powers of his office, give him great political weight. Nevertheless, he cannot do much of importance without at least the tacit cooperation of the leaders of the party that has a majority in the council. (Since council and mayor are elected at the same time, these are very likely to be the leaders of the mayor's own party.) In effect, he and the party leaders run the city government together.

Until the late 1940's Philadelphia was firmly in the Republican camp. In 1947 the Democrats nominated a "blueribbon" candidate, Richardson Dilworth, for mayor. He lost, but he became the Democrats' most effective campaigner. He remained in the news while revelations of corruption in the city government rocked the Republican administration. Then in 1949 he ran for city treasurer and his former campaign manager, Joseph S. Clark, Jr., ran for city controller. They swept the election by more than 100,000 votes. In 1951 Clark ran for mayor and Dilworth for district attorney. Again they won overwhelmingly.

The Democratic organization, however, was made unhappy by the behavior of its reform candidates once they had assumed office. They gave many good jobs to independents, and Mayor Clark insisted on enforcing the civil service provisions of the new charter.

When the 1953 primary election came up, the Democratic machine and the reformers were openly fighting each other. A coalition of ward leaders and committeemen opposed three loan propositions that Clark put on the ballot, and the loans were voted down. The mayor's political future depended largely on his spending program, and so he was forced to bargain. In return for party support of certain bond issues, he agreed not to raise taxes.

That same year the new Democratic city chairman, Congressman William J. Green, Jr., tried to amend the charter to exempt several hundred city employees from the merit system. Mayor Clark blocked the amendment in council. Two years later, when Dilworth succeeded Clark as mayor, he surprised his reform associates by supporting a new party plan to amend the civil service provisions of the charter. But of three amendments proposed by the party, two were ruled void in the courts on technical grounds, and one was defeated in a primary election. Mayor Dilworth publicly conceded that he had made a mistake in supporting the amendments.

As of the spring of 1957, the Democratic organization had not won a general election without the support of the reformers. But by this time it was entrenched in the "delivery" wards. And when in 1954 a Democratic governor was elected, the local machine was strengthened by the acquisition of something like 3,000 jobs. In the election that fall, the machine nominated for district attorney a candidate Dilworth opposed. The man was elected by 85,000 votes, and the machine leaders felt that they could now get along nicely without the reformers. They went on to win a primary contest for a vacant congressional seat, again over reform opposition.

From then until his death, Green was boss. The Democratic party controlled Philadelphia and he controlled it. A Democratic politician had nothing to gain and everything to lose by crossing him. On the local level he was the link between the mayor and the council. When he "gave the word," the council acted. His organization also had great influence in the state party. Because the state is almost evenly divided between Republicans and Democrats, a Democrat cannot win a state-wide election without the support of the Philadelphia Democratic organization. State patronage in Philadelphia was funneled through Green from 1954 until the Republicans won the governorship in 1962.

When Green unexpectedly died, a machine man, Francis R. Smith, was elected chairman of the city Democratic committee in what Senator (and former mayor) Clark called a "blitz." Smith and the mayor were expected to carry on a long struggle for control. Despite his initial stroke in winning the chairmanship, it was by no means certain that

Smith would come out on top. The powers of his office gave the mayor a formidable advantage in the long run.

What Parties and Elections Are Like

Philadelphia is divided into sixty wards, which in turn are divided into precincts or "election divisions." Both parties are organized by wards and divisions. At the bottom of the party hierarchy are 3,266 elected committeemen (in most cities they would be called "precinct captains"), two from each division. The committeemen from each ward constitute a ward committee, which elects a ward leader. The sixty ward leaders constitute a city (Democratic or Republican) committee; they elect one of their number city chairman.

About 1,500 court jobs and 300 other city jobs are exempt from the merit system. Another important source of patronage is the state. Pennsylvania has practically no merit system: 50,000 state jobs help to support local machines throughout the state. Philadelphia's share of these jobs has been estimated at from 600 to 3,000. The wide range of these estimates probably reflects different ideas of what constitutes a "job."

Only in certain parts of the city is patronage of much help to a party. In South Philadelphia, for example, ethnic ties are more important than jobs in winning the voters' favor. In some neighborhoods, a politician said, all a committeeman need do is slap a voter on the back, walk into the voting booth with him, and pull the lever. The largest Negro slums, located in North Central Philadelphia, are particularly amenable to patronage distributed by the Democratic machine.

THE REPUBLICAN ORGANIZATION

The decline of the local Republican party is sometimes explained by the "natural" Democratic allegiance of a big-city electorate. It is true that since the New Deal, Philadelphia has voted Democratic in national elections. But the Republicans' troubles have been partly organizational.

In the late 1930's and 40's there were two leading figures in the Republican machine, Austin Meehan, who controlled the thirty-fifth ward in Northeast Philadelphia, and Bill Meade, boss of the river wards. Many other ward leaders also had power enough to enable them to deal as equals with these two. Neither of the principal factions could therefore achieve effective control. Democratic opposition began to be effective in the late 1940's but the Republican leaders continued to fight each other.

Other factors also tended to diminish Republican power. After World War II many Philadelphians were dissatisfied with local politics and government. Big businessmen withdrew their support from the Republican coalition in 1948, apparently because they had lost confidence in its leaders and were discouraged by the persistent factionalism. When scandals were uncovered in city hall, middle-class voters turned against the coalition; charges of links between elected officials and the rackets made a particularly strong impression. During the administrations of the reform mayors, Clark and Dilworth, the Republicans appeared to have reconciled themselves to minority party status. Eventually a group of upper-class Republicans made a well-financed effort to capture control of the organization. They failed dismally: only one of the sixty ward leaders defected to them, and, after being beaten in the primary election in 1962, their organization folded. The next year, when the party gave its nomination for mayor to a man who was little known (he was a thirty-six-year-old Catholic who had run unsuccessfully for the council), there were whispers that its leaders had made a deal with the Democrats. Republican leaders denied this emphatically, however, and claim that they are rebuilding the organization at a rapid rate and have high hopes of winning the next election.

THE DEMOCRATIC PARTY

The Democratic organization was born in the 1930's and nursed on federal patronage. In its early years it also depended heavily on big contributions from a few "fat cats." One of these was John B. Kelly, the father of Princess Grace, who ran for mayor in 1935. As Boss Green built his organization, the influence of Kelly and the other "fat cats" declined. Green himself, as chairman of the city Democratic committee, became almost the whole show. It was part of his strategy to recruit ward and precinct leaders from the declining Republican machine. According to one Republican politician, the "bulk" of the present Democratic committeemen—"around 1,200 to 1,300"—are former Republicans. Some switched their allegiance immediately after Clark's victory in 1951; most, however, came over in 1954 when the election of a Democratic governor put their state jobs in jeopardy.

ELECTIONS

Municipal elections are held in odd-numbered years. The mayor, city councilmen, sheriff, city commissioner, and clerk of quarter sessions are elected at four-year intervals (1959, 1963, and so on), and the controller, district attorney, and registrar of wills in the other odd-numbered years (1957, 1961, 1965). These last are called "row office" elections. Judges and magistrates are elected in all odd-numbered years.

Party primaries are held on the second Tuesday in May, except in presidential election years, when they are held on the last Tuesday in April. Pennsylvania uses the closed primary. In order to get on the ballot, a candidate for nomination to a city-wide office (including the district committee) must file a petition signed by at least 100 electors of his party. A candidate for nomination as magistrate must get 3,000 signatures. There is a $25 filing fee.

On November 6, 1962, 1,003,070 voters were registered. Voter turnout since World War II has been about 90 per cent of registration in presidential elections, 75 per cent in gubernatorial elections, 70 per cent in mayoralty elections, 57 per cent in row office elections, and 20 to 25 per cent in primaries.

Before 1949 the "controlled vote" (lower-class) wards were solidly Republican in local elections. But in the 1949 row office election, the Democrats, with their "blue-ribbon" slate, carried not only the "independent" wards but also most lower-class wards. Apparently the GOP machine functioned badly because of factional feuds. At any rate, the Democrats polled a far higher percentage of their registration than the Republicans did of theirs. In the 1951 mayoralty election the same thing happened.

James H. J. Tate became mayor in 1962 when Dilworth resigned to run (unsuccessfully) for governor. The next year Tate ran for his first full term against a little-known lawyer. The election was regarded as a test of sentiment toward New Frontier racial policies (President Kennedy flew to Philadelphia the week before the election to endorse Tate). Negro voters had given strong support to both Clark and Dilworth, but in this election the machine was caught between militant Negroes who felt Tate had not gone far enough and resentful whites who felt that the Democrats (President Kennedy, if not Mayor Tate) had gone too far. Republicans charged Tate with being "Green's mayor" and said his administration was corrupt. Party workers on both sides noticed signs of hostility to the Democrats in normally Democratic wards. But the returns proved that the organization is still on top. Negroes and working-class whites gave Tate a heavy vote, and he won by a margin of 64,000 (as compared with Clark's 124,800 in 1951 and Dilworth's 133,000 in 1955 and 207,000 in 1959). The Democrats also retained control of the city council. Many people gave Green and his organization credit for the victory.

Interest Groups and Influentials

BUSINESS

Until the end of World War II, a "Main Line," old-family business elite (railroads, banks, insurance, and utilities especially) shared actively in the management of the Republican city machine. The machine depended upon the businessmen for financial support and so, to a large extent, did the city administrations. Throughout the 1930's and early 40's the city government was in bad financial straits. In 1939 the bankers loaned it $41 million, taking in return the revenues of the city-owned gas works. Some of them also made direct financial contributions. A decade later, alarmed at the city's continued decline, the "Main Line" businessmen withdrew their support from the Republican machine, thus preparing the way for its collapse and the election of the reformers on the Democratic ticket.

At present the business elite's influence is exercised mainly through the Greater Philadelphia Movement (GPM). This is a nonprofit corporation organized in 1948 and dominated by lawyers and bankers, most of them "old family." GPM has been particularly active in planning and renewal matters. The Dock Street food distribution center, which Mayor Dilworth financed with a multi-million dollar loan over the objections of the city council, was one of its projects.

The Chamber of Commerce of Greater Philadelphia is more generally representative of business; at any rate, it is not dominated by the "Main Line" elite. Whereas GPM's influence is chiefly with the administration, the chamber's is chiefly with the city council. The "issue-oriented" style of the reformers put the chamber somewhat at a disadvantage; it was less successful than GPM in representing its projects as "in the public interest." GPM is thought of as "a group of civic leaders" and the chamber as a "pressure group." The chamber can nevertheless point to a number of accomplishments. One is the Philadelphia Industrial Corporation, a quasi-public body which the city government provided with a revolving fund to enable it to prepare land for acquisition by industry. The idea, of course, is to encourage industry to come to Philadelphia.

THE PRESS

Nearly everybody in Philadelphia reads one of three newspapers. The evening *Bulletin* has a daily circulation of 718,-167 and a Sunday circulation of 702,577. The morning *Inquirer* (daily circ. 603,438; Sunday, 983,643) and the afternoon tabloid *News* (circ. 317,612) are part of the Annenberg interests, which also include several profitable racing sheets, *TV Guide,* and the magazine *Seventeen.* Since one is a morning and the other an evening paper, the *Inquirer* and the *Bulletin* are not seriously in competition. This permits them to neglect sexy murders and the like in favor of serious news. Both papers are staunch supporters of "good government" (they campaigned for a home-rule charter in

1951) and both are dependable forums for the city's many civic associations. Both are Republican in state and national affairs and both used to be so in local affairs as well. From 1947, however, neither paper supported the Republicans in a local election until 1963, when the *Bulletin* backed Tate's opponent.

LABOR

Organized labor is represented on almost all important committees, both public and private, concerned with public policy. But labor representatives are too few in number to have much weight, and they are usually selected to play "representative" rather than "leadership" roles. As a rule, they take back seats unless the issue is a "bread and butter" one; then they become vocal, but usually to no avail.

Except for the Teamsters, the unions are solidly Democratic. They get few favors from the Democratic administration, however. Clark, for example, flatly refused to appoint a labor man to his cabinet, although the unions had endorsed his candidacy. Apparently the Democrats feel they can afford to cold-shoulder the unions because the unions cannot deliver any votes. They have no precinct organization, and their members pay little or no attention to the endorsements they make. Some sectors of the electorate, on the other hand, are fearful of union domination. It is in order to put such fears to rest, perhaps, that the Democrats tend conspicuously to ignore the unions. However this may be, the unions nevertheless contribute substantially to the party's local campaign—usually about $50,000 and sometimes much more, it is said. Labor, a businessman remarked, buys protection from the party in power for the same reasons that business does.

NEGROES

Race relations in Philadelphia seem to be somewhat better than in most large Northern cities. One reason for this, perhaps, is the presence in the city of a quarter of a million Jews. Another may be the interest that the powerful Democratic organization has in maintaining itself and winning elections. The extension of the merit system by the reform-

ers opened thousands of city jobs to Negroes. This not only
attached the Negro to the Democratic party but also, in all
likelihood, improved his morale. The reformers were not
the only ones to take an interest in the Negro, however.
Green put Negro candidates on the slate for Congress, the
Common Pleas Court and the city council, and he saw to it
that they were appointed to important posts, including the
Civil Service Commission. His successors will undoubtedly
follow the same policy.

For a long time the Philadelphia chapter of the NAACP
was under the wing of the Fellowship Commission, a predominantly Jewish group devoted to brotherhood ("Let's all
live by the Golden Rule"). Several years ago, after a change
of leadership, it emerged as a lively, independent force
claiming 20,000 members. In 1961 it charged the school
board with gerrymandering school districts and discriminat-
ing against Negro teachers. The next year it threatened to
boycott the Ford Motor Company if the Philadelphia Council for Community Advancement, the recipient of a $1.7
million Ford Foundation grant to attack social problems, did
not replace the Jew it had appointed as its executive director with a Negro.

The Negro Trade Union Leadership Council, composed
of several hundred Negro union officials, is said to have a
good deal of influence among Negroes, both because Philadelphia unions are integrated and because many Negroes see
something to hope for from a Negro-labor alliance.

How Issues Are Handled

When the Republicans were in power one of their main
boasts was that they kept taxes, particularly property taxes,
down. The level of city services was correspondingly low, of
course, and the city was constantly in financial trouble.
There was no doubt, however, that many people approved
of the low tax rate. The reform mayors, Clark and Dilworth,
chose to make their record by improving services, which
meant that they would also have to raise taxes. In his campaign for reelection in 1959, Dilworth warned that he
meant to raise taxes in order to improve services. He carried

fifty-eight wards and won by a record plurality. He then announced that he wanted an additional $96 million in revenue for use over a four-year period.

To get the money he had to have council approval. Fifteen of the seventeen councilmen were Democrats, and these always voted in accordance with a majority decision taken at a caucus. It was very soon clear that Dilworth did not have the eight votes he needed. Some Democrats on the council thought that the public did not want improved services enough to pay for them. Others were against paying for them, as the mayor proposed to do, with a wage tax. Still others were opposed to spending huge sums on urban renewal (the kind of thing that the liberals and downtown businessmen who were the mayor's chief supporters wanted). The mayor followed the usual procedure for such an impasse: he appointed a tax-study commission consisting of seven downtown businessmen and bankers, a labor leader, two councilmen, and his director of finance. The council ignored the commission and proceeded at once to cut the mayor's $96-million request by more than half and to express opposition to any wage tax.

The tax-study commission went ahead, however. It hired a highly respectable, business-dominated, tax-conscious body to make a study for it, on the basis of which it recommended a tax increase of $65 million, slightly more than half of which would come from a wage tax. The labor representative on the commission dissented vigorously. The city should spend an additional $90 million, he said, and the money should come from taxes that would fall most heavily on the rich.

The press and the business organizations supported the commission's recommendation. The Chamber of Commerce, which had opposed the mayor's initial request, was willing to settle for the $65-million figure. So was the Board of Realtors. The mayor got the support of the AFL by pointing out that most of the money would go to urban renewal, which would provide work for the building trades, and to raise the salaries of city employees. Later, by offering the Municipal Workers Union a modified closed shop, he brought all of the major unions into line.

He still did not have the eight Democratic votes he needed on the council. To get them he traveled to Washington for a confidential talk with Congressman Green, the chairman of the Democratic City Committee. Apparently he made three concessions to Green as the price for the needed votes: he would let an organization man be cochairman of the Citizens for Kennedy, he would reduce the amount of the proposed wage tax slightly, and he would recommend increasing the salaries of the councilmen from $12,000 to $15,000. These arrangements having been made, the fifteen Democrats on the council voted unanimously for the modified tax proposal and the two Republicans voted against it.

ST. LOUIS:

Better Than She Should Be

Generally speaking, upper-income people tend to support reform and "good government" and lower-income people tend to be indifferent or downright hostile to them. St. Louis has fewer upper-income and more lower-income people (in proportion to total population) than any other big city outside the South; it should therefore be one of the worst-governed cities in the United States. In fact, the structure of its political system is unreformed; St. Louis is one of the few big cities where elections are partisan and where aldermen represent wards. The functioning of the system, however, is exactly the opposite of what one would expect. The city's government is characterized by the very virtues—honesty, efficiency, and impartiality—reformers cherish most. To these rather paradoxical facts, another must be added: a generation or so ago St. Louis was predominantly middle class—and notoriously corrupt.

Population and Economy

In the last twenty years, the middle class has moved from the city to the suburbs at a rapid rate. Southern Negroes and "mountain" whites have moved in, some to stay and others to pass on after a few months or years to places further north. Despite this in-migration, the net loss of population has been considerable: 13 per cent between 1950 and 1960. Of the 750,000 people who lived in the city in 1960, 29 per cent were Negro, as opposed to only 18 per cent ten years earlier.

Germans are the largest foreign-stock group, with Italians and Irish next. Most of the Germans and the Irish are third- and fourth-generation; for this reason, perhaps, nationality ties are of little importance in politics. Religious affiliations are more important. About one-third of the whites in the city are Catholic. The Jewish population is small—roughly 1 per cent of the total.

St. Louis is supported by highly diversified industry—"a huge industrial department store," it has been called. Like other midwestern cities, however, it does not have many new, science-based industries, and there are some who say its prospects for industrial and commercial growth in the next decade are not good.

How the Government Is Organized

St. Louis has the strong-mayor-council form of government. The mayor is elected for a four-year term and is the chief executive of the government. A Board of Aldermen consists of twenty-eight members elected from wards and a president elected at large. The aldermen serve four-year terms; half of them are elected every two years.

The mayor, the comptroller (also elected for a four-year term), and the president of the Board of Aldermen together form the Board of Estimate and Apportionment. This body prepares the budget, which the Board of Aldermen may cut but not increase. The mayor appoints all department heads. Seven of the principal department heads together form a Board of Public Service, which prepares and recommends all ordinances for public works, lets construction contracts, and grants certain permits.

THE COUNTY

The city of St. Louis does not lie within any county. (There is a St. Louis County, but it adjoins the city to the west.) Functions normally performed by county governments in Missouri are performed for the area of the city of St. Louis by officials (sheriff, collector of revenue, license collector, and recorder of deeds) chosen by the same electorate that chooses city officials. The officials who perform county functions are entirely independent of the city officials, however.

SCHOOLS

The Board of Education, consisting of twelve members elected for six-year terms, is also independent. The school district tax rate is fixed in a special referendum.

POLICE

The police department is run by a board of five commissioners, the mayor and four others appointed by the governor. The city is required by law to raise whatever revenue the Board of Police Commissioners requires for the support of the department.

THE ELECTORATE

Bond issues go before the electorate and must be approved by a two-thirds majority of those voting.

How It Really Works

Despite this wide distribution of authority, the mayor is the principal force in the city government. His power does not rest on patronage: of the city's approximately 10,000 jobs, all but about twenty-five are under civil service. But because as mayor he is closer to the center of things than either of the other two members of the Board of Estimate and Apportionment, he plays the leading part in the preparation of the budget. This gives him a decided advantage in dealing with the Board of Aldermen; even when a majority of it is hostile to him, he has the upper hand.

The county officials, the Board of Education, the Board of Police Commissioners, and the Election Commissioners all have a good deal of patronage at their disposal. (The Board of Education, for example, spends $2 million a year for maintenance workers.) This gives these bodies real, as well as legal and formal, independence. They seldom try to interfere in affairs that are under the mayor's jurisdiction, and he knows better than to try to interfere in matters that are under theirs.

The elected officials, together with their principal subordinates, form two quite separate sets. The Mayor's Office

Group consists of those with responsibility for making and carrying out policy. The mayor is at the center of this group, of course, and the two elected officials who share responsibility with him for the preparation of the budget usually stand close to him in it. The Mayor's Office Group stands for "good government" and "civic progress." Its chief supporters are the newspapers, the downtown business interests, and the middle-class wards. Its policies, however, are not always conservative; in race relations and even in fiscal matters it has often been innovative and progressive.

The other set, the County Office Group, consists of county officials and some aldermen. They have little to do with policy. They are "politicians" in the narrow sense; their main interest is in getting and giving jobs and favors. Their base of support consists of Negroes, small businessmen, the politically active elements of organized labor, and the low-income wards.

Elected committeemen control party organization in the wards and can in some cases decide who is to be alderman. The County Office Group has enough patronage to tie the committeemen into a machine that might control the city. Instead of pooling their patronage to do this, however, the various elements within the County Office Group bid against each other for the committeemen's support. This makes it possible for the committeemen to maintain their independence (one who refuses to knuckle under to one element of the County Office Group cannot be well disciplined, for a competing element is always at hand with an attractive alternative) and in effect it guarantees that a diverse set of interests will be represented on the Board of Aldermen. Consequently the mayor is seldom confronted by a large, stable opposition bloc within the board.

When they join forces, the County Office Group and the ward leaders can usually make or break a candidate for the state legislature. The mayor, on the other hand, having no patronage, can do nothing to help a candidate. When measures brought forward by the city administration are blocked in the legislature, it is usually the County Office Group that is responsible, not, as outsiders usually suppose, hostile rural influence.

Normally the relationship between the Mayor's Office Group and the County Office Group is of the kind game theorists call "cooperative conflict." Neither side is strong enough to put the other out of business, and each needs the other to survive. The Mayor's Office Group needs help in the machine-contolled wards on election day. The County Office Group needs campaign contributions from downtown businessmen. Sometimes, as will appear below, certain vital interests of the two groups come in conflict. When this happens, there is a resounding crash. The rule, however, is peaceful coexistence.

How They Get Elected

St. Louis had Republican administrations for a quarter of a century before the New Deal and again from 1941 to 1949. Today only four wards are reliably Republican. Most precincts are without precinct captains or workers. The changed composition of the population accounts in part for these changes. There is no doubt that more Republicans than Democrats moved out to the suburbs; of the Negroes and Southern whites who have come to the city, practically all are Democrats. But even if there had been no change in the composition of the population, the city would probably have turned Democratic anyway. In the old days the Republicans maintained their control by the methods of machine politics—that is, by buying votes with jobs, favors, and sometimes money. Except in the lowest-income wards, these methods have long been unacceptable and unworkable. And in the lowest-income wards, the Democrats' identification with the welfare state gives them an advantage which the Republicans would find hard to offset even if they could—and would—distribute "gravy" as of old. The Democrats, on the other hand, can use jobs and favors to strengthen their natural advantage in these wards. Half a dozen wards on the north side and along the river are known as "delivery" wards. These get a considerable amount of patronage and contribute substantially to Democratic victories. The amount of patronage available is declining year by year, however, and the number of deliverable votes is falling off accordingly. To carry the city, the Democrats must now get a heavy vote in the middle-income wards on the south side ("newspaper" wards, as they are called); the only way to do so is to establish a record that appeals to the good government-minded.

This mutuality of interest between "delivery" and "newspaper" wards results in the election of "good government"-minded mayors. For 16 years beginning in 1949 the mayor was a former professor of mechanical engineering at Washington University named Raymond R. Tucker. Tucker was a Democrat, but not a party professional, and his style was that of a city manager rather than a politician. He suited the newspapers, the businessmen, and the middle-class and home-owning voters who wanted honesty, efficiency, impartiality, and "civic progress," but he bored and irritated the professional politicians and many of the working-class voters. ("In politics," a politician said, "there are two kinds of people you have to watch out for—professors and military men. They seem to think that they can go around giving orders to people. Mayor Tucker . . . thinks he can give orders and get things done.") In the primary of 1965, the voters decided it was time for a change. Tucker was badly beaten by A. J. Cervantes, a businessman (he is in kinds of business—insurance and taxicabs, for example—which often benefit from political connections) and former alderman who was supported by most of the ward leaders. In the runoff, Cervantes beat his Republican opponent by a more than 2 to 1 margin.

In the primary Tucker failed to get much support from Negroes, despite his outstanding record in race relations. Lower-middle-class whites, many of whom considered the city's big urban renewal program an extravagance, also turned to Cervantes in large numbers. Some said that the primary vote represented a repudiation not only of Tucker but of the whole "good government" establishment—the newspapers, the university, and the big business-civic leadership crowd that had helped Tucker raze the downtown core of the city with urban renewal—and they looked for a return to corrupt, machine-style government. It is more likely, however, that Cervantes (who incidentally was supported by Tucker, the newspapers, and the "good government" forces in general when he ran for president of the board of aldermen in 1959) will try hard to equal Tucker's record for "good government." He will need to pick up strength in the "newspaper" wards just as Tucker needed to pick it up in the "delivery" ones. Moving from an opposite direction, so to speak, he is likely to end up very near where Tucker was.

How long this alliance can be maintained is a question. If the city continues to lose middle-class and gain working-class voters, the time will come when the "newspaper" wards will not be needed to insure a Democratic victory. By then, however, a considerable part of the working class may have moved into the middle class or, at any rate, have come to value the "good government" virtues. In this event, St. Louis may go on having what amounts to an elected city manager.

Interest Groups and Influentials

NEGROES

The Negro community has long had many channels through which to make its influence felt. Thanks to the ward-based electoral system, six Negroes sit on the Board of Aldermen and two on the Board of Education. There is a strong NAACP and an active Urban League. The newspapers have for many years taken an active interest in racial problems. A number of churches, both white and Negro, have social action groups. The Roman Catholic archdiocese, the Rabbinical Association, and the Metropolitan Church Federation have worked together on public accommodations questions. An Advisory Committee on Race Relations appointed by the mayor meets with him regularly.

These efforts have led to a good deal of action. The Board of Education has made vigorous efforts to desegregate and improve the schools. (Catholic schools were desegregated by order of the Archbishop as early as 1946.) In 1961 the mayor managed, by much skillful behind-the-scenes work, to get an important public accommodations bill passed.

Later he convened a Commission on Equal Employment
Opportunity. This recommended a nine-point program
which Downtown, Inc., an association of businessmen,
urged upon its members. In the view of most Negro leaders,
the main problems now have to do with jobs and housing.
The basis of the job problem is lack of heavy industry to
employ unskilled and semi-skilled workers; competition between Negroes and Southern whites for the places left by
people who move to the suburbs is the basis of the housing
problem.

Events in other cities have tended to discredit the moderate approach of the established Negro leaders and to cast
doubt on the value of what has been done through negotiation. According to CORE, the St. Louis leader of which is a
young (twenty-seven years old in 1964) white graduate of
Washington University, Mayor Tucker's program represented "half a loaf." The Negroes, this man says, are fed up
with the traditional organization of local political parties
along patronage lines.

THE TEAMSTERS

Of the approximately 35,000 Teamsters who live in St.
Louis, about one-fourth belong to Local 688, Warehouse and
Distribution Workers. The size of this union, the distribution of its membership (there are few wards that do not
have a considerable number of Local 688 men), and the
extraordinary energy and ability of its secretary-treasurer
have made it an important interest group. Through its
"Community Action Stewards' Assembly," Local 688 tries
to apply "shop" procedures to ward and city matters. In
every ward a community action steward is elected for
twenty-five members of the local who live there. "Community grievances" are reported by the members to their
stewards who investigate, confer with the alderman, or take
whatever action seems appropriate. Twice a year the steward and his members meet with the alderman to discuss
ward problems. Once a month stewards from all over the
city get together at union headquarters to talk about city
problems and to pass requests from the ward meetings on
to higher authorities.

The union is interested in a wide range of matters. A report of the resolutions committee of one Annual City-Wide Shop Conference criticized the police department, called for a graduated income tax, opposed an increase in the earnings tax, favored metropolitan government, protested a cut-back in garbage collection, and threatened legal action if the city did not enforce its air pollution control ordinance. Some observers think the Teamsters' influence is on the wane. Efforts to organize ward machines have failed, and the new militancy of some Negroes is stealing thunder from the unions.

BUSINESS

A principal element in the "good government," "civic progress" coalition is downtown business. The large retailers, utilities, banks, and insurance companies jointly support a public relations and promotions office ("at Christmas we had strolling minstrels . . . and at Easter girls in bunny costumes distributing balloons. And we've put trash baskets on the corners."). A much more serious effort, Civic Progress, Inc., has helped get bond issues passed and has provided leadership and financial support for efforts at charter reform, governmental reorganization, and urban renewal. These activities have led to an improvement of relations between the business community and the Board of Aldermen. After ten years of accomplishment, however, Civic Progress, Inc., seems to be running out of things to do.

THE PRESS

Although Joseph Pulitzer does not participate in local affairs much himself, his paper, the evening *Post-Dispatch* (daily circ. 344,575; Sunday, 569,578) maintains the tradition of civic leadership established by its founder. Richard Amberg, publisher of the morning *Globe-Democrat* (daily circ. 295,004; Sunday, 355,183), is personally more involved on the local scene, but his newspaper has less influence than the *Post-Dispatch*. Both newspapers supported the Tucker forces and are probably very helpful in getting out the vote in the middle-class wards. The high quality of the Tucker administration tended to frustrate the newspapers' natural taste for civic crusading. "We don't look hard for embarrassing things," a reporter remarked. Now that Cervantes is mayor, they probably will.

How Issues Are Handled

The difficulty of bringing about any change that would upset the balance of power among the principal interests within the city and the metropolitan area may be seen from the failure of repeated efforts at governmental reorganization. St. Louis City cut itself off from the County of St. Louis by constitutional provision in 1876 in order to safeguard itself from corrupt "courthouse politics." Before long, however, it was chafing at its boundaries. After World War II, downtown businessmen began to look for ways of renewing the central city. At this same time, the middle-class, "good government" wing of the Democratic party was beginning to worry about the changes that were taking place in the composition of the electorate. The businessmen and the good-government-minded politicians saw that there would be advantages in some kind of reunion of the city with the county. In 1950 an elected Board of Freeholders proposed a revision of the city charter. The reformers wanted to create a broader taxing authority, thus increasing revenue for the support of municipal services, and they wanted also to strike a blow at machine politics. They proposed centralizing authority under the mayor, eliminating much of the county office patronage, putting the county offices under the mayor's fiscal control, and levying an earnings tax. The daily newspapers and the businessmen quickly endorsed these proposals. All but one of the ward politicians opposed them, however, as did the Teamsters and most of the Negro leaders. When it came to a vote, the proposed charter was badly beaten.

Out of the ashes of this defeat sprang the businessman's organization, Civic Progress, Inc. In 1956, after waging a successful campaign for the earnings tax and for two bond issues, it led another attempt at charter revision. The new plan was to reduce the influence of "politicians" and "special interests" by reducing the size of the Board of Aldermen and electing half of it at large. This plan also was defeated at the polls. Negroes (who would lose representation), organized labor, some ward leaders, neighborhood businesses, and the community press were all against it.

Almost immediately a more ambitious reorganization was proposed. With a large grant, the Ford Foundation created the Metropolitan St. Louis Survey, which made two studies. One was an elaborate public opinion poll intended to reveal widespread popular dissatisfaction with city and county services but showing in fact that most people were fairly well satisfied with things as they were. The other recommended creation of a multi-purpose metropolitan district government. After much debate, an elected Board of Freeholders voted 10 to 9 to offer a plan of this kind to the voters. It proposed creation of a Greater St. Louis City-County District to be run by a president and council of twelve, elected on a nonpartisan basis, to administer certain area-wide functions (roads, planning, transportation, sewage, drainage, civil defense, property assessment, and economic development). Again the daily newspapers and the businessmen approved and again the other principal interests disapproved. Some opponents, among them the Negroes, felt that the plan went too far. Others, including organized labor, thought it did not go far enough. Only three of the twenty-eight Democratic ward organizations favored the reorganization. Neither the Democratic nor the Republican county organizations took a stand, but county politicians in both parties worked against it. Late in the campaign, Mayor Tucker came out against the plan. It would not work, he said, and it would make bad matters worse by increasing the complexity of government organization. In the city the voters turned the plan down 2 to 1; in the county they turned it down 3 to 1.

The reformers then made still another proposal: to abolish 115 governmental units and establish in their place a single city government with jurisdiction over a population of 1,500,000 and an area larger than that of any city in the United States. The new city would be divided into twenty-two boroughs, each of which would elect two members of a governing council. This plan, which was endorsed by Mayor

Tucker, necessitated a constitutional amendment and so had to be voted on by the whole state. It was defeated by a 6-to-5 margin in the city, a 4-to-1 margin in the county, and a 3-to-1 margin elsewhere. If the St. Louis area was to be governed well, it would have to be through organizational arrangements of which the "good government" movement thoroughly disapproved. This, of course, was the way the city had long been governed.

SEATTLE:

Anybody in Charge?

In the 1930's Seattle was probably the widest-open port in the country. Its politicians were always flamboyant and often corrupt. ("There's going to be no cheap chiseling at the City Hall. I intend to take it all myself," promised Vic Meyers, a bandleader and nightclub owner who ran for mayor in 1932.) The city had a tradition of labor radicalism and popular discontent; elections were bitterly fought along class lines, and incumbents usually lost.

In 1938 Seattle elected a reform mayor who cleaned it up thoroughly. The war then brought industry and prosperity, and the post-war years, a residential building boom. Today Seattle has more middle-class people (in proportion to population) and more prosperous ones than any other large city. Its people are busy making money, rearing children, trimming lawns, and boating, and its politics, far from being radical, corrupt, or bitter, is downright dull.

Population and Economy

Seattle's population was 557,087 in 1960, an increase of 19 per cent in the decade. It is predominantly native white. Persons of foreign stock (28 per cent of the total) come mainly from Canada, Norway, Sweden, and the United Kingdom. The Ballard district, where the first Scandinavian immigrants settled, is still the Norwegian-Swedish center, but second- and third-generation Scandinavian-Americans live all over the city. The nonwhite population is small—8.4 per cent of the total. It consists of 27,000 Negroes who are concentrated in the Capital Hill district and 14,000 Orientals scattered throughout the city. The Jewish population is very small—about 10,500 in the whole metropolitan area.

The relative homogeneity of its population, its prosperity, and the high rate of single-family home ownership give Seattle a suburban quality. As in other West Coast cities, people have strong attachments to neighborhood communities. Geography helps establish the separateness of these and identification with them is heightened by the presence of a commercial club and a weekly newspaper. The attachment to the communities is a fact that politicians have to reckon with; for example, if it is to mobilize support for a bond issue, the city government must promise each community something.

In its youth Seattle was a lumbering, mining, and fishing town; this is what made it rough and radical. World War II brought shipbuilding and aircraft industries (the Boeing Company is now the largest of the latter). Many of the aircraft workers have white-collar jobs as clerks, engineers, technicians, and managers. A high proportion of the labor force is now employed in wholesale and retail trade, public administration, finance and insurance, and real estate; these people, of course, also wear white collars. Obviously the changes that have occurred in the economic base of the city largely account for its new class character and for its sedate, if not stodgy, political style.

How the Government Is Organized

Seattle has a weak-mayor-council form of government—a legacy from its turbulent past. A new charter was discussed in 1946, but business interests and good government groups, remembering the bad old days of the 1930's, opposed any centralizing of authority, and the voters agreed.

THE MAYOR

The mayor is elected for a four-year term and is paid $23,-000. He appoints, subject to council approval, the heads of the police and fire departments for indefinite terms and he makes rules governing those departments. With the council's approval he also appoints for four-year terms the heads of the light, engineering, building, and water departments. These four officials constitute the Board of Public Works.

Their terms are staggered, and the mayor may not remove any of them without the council's consent. It follows, then, that not until near the end of his term does a mayor have the opportunity to put men of his own choice in all the departments under his control.

The mayor also appoints members of five unsalaried administrative boards and commissions—the Transit Commission, the Park Board, the Library Board, the Civil Service Commission, and the Planning Commission. Except for three ex-officio members of the Planning Commission, these appointees have staggered terms. Appointments must be approved by the council, and board members may not be removed without council consent. The boards are relatively independent of the mayor; under state law, the transit department has control of its budget and the other four departments are not required to consult the mayor before submitting budget requests to the council.

The treasurer, comptroller, and corporation counsel, all of whom are elected, also administer their departments independently of the mayor. He accordingly has little control over the city's financial and legal affairs.

There is no patronage anywhere in the city government. Except for a few department heads, all appointments are made under merit system regulations.

THE COUNCIL

The city council is powerful. Its nine members are elected at large, serve four-year terms, and are paid $10,000. Four positions on the council are contested in one election and five in the next, two years later. After each election the council selects one of its members as its president.

When a measure is brought before the council, the president refers it to a committee for study. Committee chairmen are powerful; they do most of the day-to-day work and their decisions are usually backed by the other members. The council considers them its experts on their particular subjects. Through the committees, councilmen exert a good deal of control over city departments. The chairman of the public safety committee, for example, maintains close liaison with the head of the buildings department; the department head reports to him on budgetary matters and consults with him about legislation which might affect the department.

Because of the power of the committee chairmen, department heads are inclined to pay more attention to them than to the mayor. The normal channel of public access to a department is through a council committee, not through the mayor's office.

The council has authority over most city finances. It adopts the budget for all departments except transit, and it sets rates of pay and authorizes creation of new salaried positions for all except the transit and library departments. The chairman of the finance committee controls the budget. Departments not responsible to the mayor submit their requests directly to the finance committee's budget office; the other departments go over their requests with the mayor before submitting them to the budget office.

SCHOOLS

The school district is run by a five-member board elected at large on a nonpartisan basis for four-year terms. Voter approval is required for bond issues and excess levies.

OTHER BODIES

The Port of Seattle District and the Municipality of Metropolitan Seattle, which handles sewage disposal for Seattle and some suburbs, are independent of the city government.

Kings County is governed by thirty-four elected officials, twenty-four appointed boards and commissions, and eleven appointed officials. Except for judges, elections are on a partisan basis. Three commissioners, nominated from districts but elected at large, form the nearest thing to a central executive. About 3,000 jobs are filled on a patronage basis.

THE ELECTORATE

Many matters are decided by referendum. Early in 1964, for example, the electorate acted (unfavorably) on a proposal, in the form of a charter amendment, to require the Transit Commission to buy trolleys rather than buses.

How It Really Works

"Seattle is governed," a city official has said, "by a network of little administrative hierarchies, each with a council committee at its apex." The main factor linking the hierarchies together is the influence of the council president. For many years, one man, David Levine, held this post. Without his agreement it was almost impossible to get anything done. He retired in 1962, and the network of little hierarchies has been looser since.

Levine's theory, to which the council still holds, was that government should do as little as possible. Councilmen think that balancing the budget is their main job, and they are very reluctant to embark on new programs. "Whenever we want something done," a civic leader said, "we must accomplish it in spite of the council."

Seattle mayors have to choose between fighting the council and getting nothing done and playing second fiddle to it and getting little done. Mayor Allen Pomeroy (1952-56) chose the first course. The council withheld approval from some of his appointments (quixotic ones, to be sure) and he retaliated by vetoing certain ordinances. After a long struggle he left office without having accomplished much. His successor, Gordon Clinton (1956-64), chose the second course and had somewhat better success. At his suggestion the council hired consultants to survey city administration, and some changes came from this. Later he got the council to approve a six-year capital improvements program and then persuaded the voters to approve a bond issue to carry it out. All this gave the impression that he was a strong mayor. Actually, however, the council had him on a short tether; his main talent was for negotiation with it. Mayor J. D. Braman, who took office in April, 1964, had been before his election the only strong figure in the council. In his campaign he said that although he would not object to charter changes to strengthen the office of mayor, he was sure he could be a strong mayor without them. Braman, a *Seattle Times* reporter wrote, is a "direct actionist who . . . pursues his objectives with boundless and often impatient energy." Whether even a direct activist can dominate so profoundly inactivist a council remains to be seen.

How They Get Elected

THE NONPARTISAN SYSTEM

Seattle elections have been nonpartisan and at large since 1910, when during a wave of reform a charter amendment was placed on the ballot by initiative petition. Until 1938 nonpartisanship existed in name only. Since then, both parties have normally refrained from making endorsements, giving financial help to candidates, or furnishing party workers on election day. There have been exceptions, however. The Democratic organization helped elect Pomeroy mayor, and in 1964, when Lieutenant Governor John A. Cherberg opposed J. D. Braman for mayor, the Democrats worked for him and the Republicans for Braman. Nevertheless, since 1936 the mayors of Seattle have not been party politicians.

The 3,000 employees of Kings County are not under a merit system. But patronage has not been used to build party machines; instead, the various county officials have used it to build personal followings. Some of these "organizations" have only nominal ties with the parties.

ELECTIONS

Municipal elections are held in February of even-numbered years, and the general election is held two weeks later, in March. In the decade 1950-60, the percentage of registered voters actually voting in municipal elections ranged from 20.0 to 49.3 in the primaries and from 42.0 to 65.3 in the general elections. By contrast, in state and national elections, the percentage was from 30.7 to 54.4 in the primaries and from 63.2 to 79.3 in the general elections.

Success in a council election depends largely upon making one's name known. To do this a council candidate builds up ties in his own neighborhood and then extends them by joining city-wide organizations and making frequent public appearances. His party affiliation is rarely known to the general public. Nor are issues important. Council candidates build popularity with public appearances and platitudes.

Once elected, a councilman usually can keep his job for life. Incumbents have an advantage that is seldom overcome: in sixty-five contests for council positions in sixteen elections between 1940 and 1964, incumbents were defeated only five times. Usually the incumbents campaign as a team and stress their record of "fiscal responsibility," each pointing with pride to the record of the committee he heads. Usually the incumbents do best in the higher-income districts; the challengers do best in the lower-income areas.

Recruitment of candidates for council, fund-raising, and campaign organization are in the hands of interest groups, civic organizations, and newspapers. Editorial endorsements by neighborhood weekly papers probably have more influence than do those of the daily press, for the weeklies usually give a good deal of publicity to the one or two candidates who are local residents. Each council candidate depends upon a circle of friends to help him conduct his campaign. Campaigns are not expensive; they are financed mainly by small contributions from interest groups. A successful candidate, however, has no doubt that he owes his election less to these groups than to his own efforts. A defeated candidate, on the other hand, may owe his defeat to others. In the 1964 council election, for example, the radical right distributed a four-page flyer accusing two candidates of being directors of the American Civil Liberties Union. ("The ACLU is a DEFENDER of the COMMUNIST PARTY. Should the ACLU Control Seattle?") Sixty-five thousand copies of the flyer are said to have been distributed in the last ten days of the campaign, and some of the material in the flyers was also used in newspaper advertisements. Both of the candidates affiliated with the ACLU lost, though not necessarily because of their affiliation with it (they were also supporters of an unpopular open occupancy proposal on the same ballot, and they had the disadvantage of being challengers rather than incumbents).

In mayoralty elections, the candidates' party affiliations—normally very lukewarm ones—are known to the voters, who probably take them into account to some extent. The vote tends to divide along the same socio-economic and geographic lines as in partisan (county, state, and national) elections. However, this does not signify that party affiliation is of much importance. In fact, although the Democrats have had a majority in Seattle all the time, Pomeroy is the only Democrat to have been elected mayor since 1938.

Reform came to Seattle under business and church auspices, and these influences have been important in elections ever since. In 1934 a group of young businessmen, most of them Republicans, formed the New Order of Cincinnatus to clean the grafters and radicals out of City Hall. With the help of workers from the Greater Seattle Council of Churches, the Cincinnatans elected several councilmen, one of whom, Arthur Langlie, was swept into the mayor's chair by a landslide reform vote in 1938. Langlie soon went on to be governor, but he and his successor made a good start at cleaning up the city. In 1942 the business and Protestant church groups (the Cincinnatans had by now disbanded), assisted by the press, elected a young lawyer, William F. Devin. He served for ten years and finished the job the others had begun. The Democrats now professed to believe that nonpartisanship was nothing more than a disguise concealing Republican control. They supported Pomeroy, who, on his second try, edged out Devin by a very small margin. Pomeroy himself was defeated four years later by Clinton, who represented a return to the reform type (he was thirty-five years old, a church and boy scout leader, and a former FBI agent and deputy prosecutor). "One Thousand Young Men for Clinton"—most of them recruited through the Council of Churches and the Young Republican Club, and much resembling the old Cincinnatans—handed out literature at downtown bus stops and made speeches to all who would listen. The Protestant churches also figured importantly in this campaign. Bundles of campaign literature were taken to some of them for distribution, and the week before the election twenty-five ministers attended a well-publicized breakfast in honor of candidate Clinton. In 1964, when Clinton decided not to run again, the business-Young Republican-Protestant church-middle-of-the-road coalition supported Braman, who had been a businessman before he became a council leader. The presence on the ballot of the proposed open housing ordinance seemed for a time to threaten the coalition. When Braman failed to support the proposal, Clinton and the Council of Churches withdrew their support from him. As it turned out, however, the clergy and the lay leaders did not represent the opinions of their congregations; rank-and-file Protestants (and for that matter Catholics) proved to be against the housing proposal.

Issues are much more important in mayoralty than in council elections. Remembering its lurid past, Seattle is particularly sensitive about matters affecting law enforcement. Candidates for mayor are apt to charge that their opponents are favored by racketeers who want to "open the city up." In the 1964 campaign the open housing issue was probably decisive. Braman, who was against having a referendum on the question, made his opponent, who finally said he would vote for open housing, appear indecisive. The proposed ordinance proved to be unpopular (it lost 112,448 to 53,-453), and this may have saved Braman from defeat (he won 93,027 to 81,681).

Interest Groups and Influentials

BUSINESS

"If you want to get anything done in Seattle," says Ross Cunningham, political editor of the *Times,* "you get about six members of the Big Ten together and tell them it's a good project. If you convince them, you're in." The Big Ten is an informal group of downtown financiers, real estate men, and industrialists. Its representatives meet every week with Chamber of Commerce and press, radio, and television people in a "Monday Luncheon Club" to discuss city affairs. No public officials are present, but it is said that big decisions affecting the city government are sometimes made. The club was organized in the mid-1930's by business leaders who wanted to rid the city of "radical" government. They were not connected with the Cincinnatus organization, but they supported its candidates. Today the Big Ten still raises money for "good government" candidates. It is loosely allied with the "Devin group," a small set of politicians associated with the former mayor. The Big Ten's money and the Devin group's political experience are a combination that has only once been beaten.

Along with other business groups, the Big Ten promotes plans for the development of the downtown business district. In 1963 the city council approved a comprehensive plan to attract customers back from the suburban shopping centers. It calls for an expenditure of $80 million of public funds to construct an inner road around the mile-square business district.

The Chamber of Commerce sometimes leads the fight in referenda campaigns, but it does not endorse candidates.

THE PRESS

Seattle has two daily newspapers, the morning *Post-Intelligencer* (daily circ., 196,459; Sunday, 243,338) and the evening *Times* (daily circ., 226,737; Sunday, 267,958). The *"PI"* is a Hearst paper; the *Times* is owned by William Blethen, the head of an old Seattle family who has close ties with local business. The political editors of both papers are frequently consulted by the Big Ten. Neither paper makes much effort to dig below the surface of municipal affairs or to generate interest in them; even their coverage of mayoralty campaigns is usually perfunctory. The papers are said to have more influence in nonpartisan than partisan elections and more in council than in mayoral contests. It is impossible to evaluate such assertions, however, for the papers almost always endorse incumbents, who would win anyway.

LABOR

Seattle is one of the most highly unionized cities in the country, but labor has little influence in local politics. Dave Beck, the one-time boss of the Teamsters' Union, is probably as much responsible for this situation as anyone. He turned labor from left to right. Although he cultivated close relations with the business community and lavished campaign contributions on candidates who were sure to win, he made no real effort to get political power. Today the Teamsters and the Kings County Central Labor Committee both speak for organized labor, but seldom with one voice. The Teamsters give their candidates large campaign contributions and the help of their public relations organization and precinct workers. These latter seldom work very hard, however.

The Central Labor Council screens candidates for local offices and makes endorsements through its Committee on Political Education (COPE). COPE's screening committee, however, is composed of union officials who have connections with particular councilmen. Unless a challenger is known to be a partisan Democrat, the committee usually prefers the incumbent. Some unions (such as building trades, machinists, and city employees) usually make independent endorsements, but none of the endorsements makes much difference.

MUNICIPAL LEAGUE

The Municipal League of Seattle and Kings County is the most important civic organization. It raises issues, mobilizes public opinion, and brings pressure to bear upon the city council. Because its membership includes representatives of the community's strongest interest groups, as well as many prestigious individuals, it can coordinate the efforts of all to prod the city government into action.

The League's full-time staff of seven coordinates research programs and issues a weekly newsletter to more than 4,000 members, most of them business and professional people. Its eighteen standing committees carry on research and conduct hearings; frequently committee studies lead to official action. Most issues in Seattle are to some extent shaped by these committees.

A League committee interviews all candidates for city, county, and school office and rates them "superior," "above average," "average," or "below average." The ratings are published in a four-page news sheet, 40,000 copies of which are distributed before each primary and general election. The daily newspapers, some business firms, and some church groups help circulate the report and publicize the ratings.

Candidates with a record of "fiscal responsibility" are most likely to please the League. Democrats often complain that Republicans get a "better pitch" and that the League rates Democrats high only when they are certain of election. In recent years some young Democratic professionals and businessmen have joined the League, but this has not changed its character.

THE COUNCIL OF CHURCHES

Former mayor Devin and some of his old associates in city politics are influential figures in the Greater Seattle Council of Churches, the political role of which was discussed above.

How Issues Are Handled

Seattle has all of the usual problems of a large central city, but it is doing—or trying to do—less than most cities to solve them. One reason may be that its problems, although similar in kind to those of other cities, are not as serious. Being a relatively young city, Seattle's housing and other physical facilities are not badly run down. Its population, moreover, is fairly homogeneous and remarkably prosperous. These factors may encourage an optimistic, if not complacent, view of things. Racial unrest, for example, is likely to remain within bounds; therefore, little need be done about it.

Another reason why Seattle attempts little is probably to be found in the weakness of its government. The office of mayor lacks enough power to attract men who want to do very much. "No one wants to be a pacifier and a middleman," one man said. But so long as the council can check him, this is about all a mayor can possibly be. A third reason why the city attempts little is that it hates to spend money. The council hates to spend it, and so do the voters. Between 1952 and 1958, they turned down eight of the eleven bond issues that were proposed by their very conservative government.

One can see how the Seattle government works—or fails to work—from its financial situation. Despite the council's record of parsimony and despite the city's having the highest median family income of any large city in the country, Seattle gets much of its revenue from small, hard-to-collect charges that fall especially heavily upon people with low incomes: traffic fines, parking-meter collections, street-use fees, meat inspection fees, and the like. For a long while the School District was also in financial straits. The PTA and the teachers association roused public opinion about this situation, but in doing so they got little help from elected officials. In general the officials watch from the sidelines while the citizens' groups struggle to get more money for public services. In their own lobbying the officials concentrate on defeating measures that would impose costs upon the city: getting new revenue for it is of secondary interest to them.

With the city government unable or unwilling to act, leadership has fallen to interest groups, "good government" organizations, and *ad hoc* citizens associations. Mayor Clinton was at his best when serving as a broker between the citizens' groups and the council. Even then, however, the initiative had to come from the citizens' groups. This is what happened when the Municipality of Metropolitan Seattle (which handles sewage disposal) was formed. The idea originated in studies by a committee of the Municipal League. When Mayor Clinton took office, he set up an official citizens' advisory committee to deal with the matter. This committee persuaded the legislature to pass enabling legislation. Then another citizens' committee campaigned for the adoption of the proposal by the electorate. About all the mayor did was to appoint the committees.

Seattle's do-it-by-citizen-committee style of government is in part the result of a charter which distributes authority so widely that neither a mayor nor anyone else can take charge. Also, the nonpartisan system gives citizens' groups more importance than they would otherwise have; if the system were partisan, the parties—and therefore the elected officials—would have to show leadership in some matters at least in order to win elections. However, these organizational factors reflect others still more basic—especially the relatively homogeneous and middle-class character of the city. At any rate it seems likely that if Seattle were as deeply divided along class, ethnic, and other lines as most large cities, it could not be governed by citizen-committees; the elected officials would in this case have to play dominant roles, either as mediators of the conflicting interests or as the agents of whatever interests were dominant. Whatever the importance of these other factors may be, it seems clear that doing-it-by-citizen-committee is highly congenial to the Protestant middle class. Whether it accomplishes anything or not, they like it this way.

Index